Minutes of Grace
Heart-to-Heart Prayers by Teens

D0725813

Edited by Laurie Delgatto-Whitten

saint mary's press

The editor for this project was Laurie Delgatto-Whitten. Prepress and manufacturing coordinated by the production departments of Saint Mary's Press.

Cover image: © Nik Merkulov / shutterstock.com

Printed in the United States of America

5040

ISBN 978-1-59982-654-7

Dedication

For Kase.
My life is so much better because you and your dad are in it.

Acknowledgments

For more than two decades, Saint Mary's Press has been publishing the written works of teens. This commitment to giving voice to our young Church, a hallmark of Saint Mary's Press, continues with *Minutes of Grace*.

I offer my deepest thanks to the hundreds upon hundreds of young people who took the time to share their most sincere and honest prayer requests. I also thank the many youth ministers, religious educators, teachers, and parents who took on the task of inviting and encouraging their teens to participate in the project.

Finally, I give a shout out to Sara Lawrence, Heather Sutton, John Vitek, and so many of the staff at Saint Mary's Press who helped to bring this project to life.

Introduction

Let's face it: most of us do not have a significant amount of time in our day to devote to prayer and one-on-one time with God. But I don't think God is asking for hours of devotion. God recognizes your busyness and simply asks that you acknowledge his presence amidst that busyness. *Minutes of Grace* helps you to do just that, providing three opportunities each day for you to stop for a moment and communicate with God. These prayers, written by teens throughout the United States (and a few from teens in other countries), speak of their struggles, joys, fears, yearnings, loss, emptiness, needs, and hope for our world.

I invite you to commit to praying these prayers daily. I invite you to give God just a few minutes of your time and in return experience your own moments of grace.

Let us all pray,

Laurie Delgatto-Whitten

Morning Prayer

God, let me find myself in your love every day.

—Abbi, Saint Paul Church, MN

Midday Prayer

Lord, help us to help the poor.

—Orion, Saint Mary Church, MO

Evening Prayer

I offer you thanks, God, for never giving up on me when I need you most.

—Lydia, Saint Mary Church, IN

Morning Prayer

Thank you for giving me a family for loving, legs for running, a voice for singing, hands for making music, and feet for dancing.

—Jane, Cotter High School, MN

Midday Prayer

Dear God, help me to keep faith in you in the darkest of times.

—Keaton, Providence High School, IN

Evening Prayer

Dear Lord, thank you for always listening to my prayers and giving me this life that I cherish.

—Bryan, Saint Joseph's Institution International, Singapore

Morning Prayer

God, help me to stay strong and handle the pressures of school.

—Alexis, Saint Joseph Church, IN

Midday Prayer

I pray for those who are struggling with their faith, personal life, or social life. I pray for those who are having troubles.

—Jonalyn, DeLaSalle High School, MN

Evening Prayer

May each of us find comfort in knowing that God loves and watches over us.

—Guy, Saint Mary Church, IN

Morning Prayer

Lord, help me to stay focused on what's important.

—Kira, La Salle High School, MN

Midday Prayer

I pray for those struggling with drugs and alcohol; may they find the strength to seek recovery.

—Cody, MT

Evening Prayer

God, I am thankful for life.

—Billy, Saint Anne Church, ND

Morning Prayer

God, protect us as we take this journey of faith.

—Kendra, Saint Mary Church, ND

Midday Prayer

I pray for everyone who feels lost; may they remain strong and look to faith.

—Emily, Good Shepherd Church, CA

Evening Prayer

Please, Lord, light my soul on fire. Amen.

—Caitlyn, Bishop Miege High School, KS

Morning Prayer

Lord, I pray to have the confidence to practice my faith in the public eye and not worry what others think.

—Victoria, Celia Cruz High School
of Music, NY

Midday Prayer

I pray for those suffering from a feeling of spiritual desertion; may they know that they are made in the image and likeness of love.

—William, Saint Joseph Church, SC

Evening Prayer

Lord, help us to remember that we do not need anyone's approval but yours.

—Marissa, Saint Michael Church, CO

Morning Prayer

God, I pray that my education helps me to better serve you, your creation, and all your people.

—Clare, Saint Therese Church, MN

Midday Prayer

Dear God, please help us to be better Catholics and to accept others into our community.

—Nicole, Saint Catherine of
Alexandria Church, MA

Evening Prayer

Lord, I pray for an end to abortion.

—Callie, Saint Patrick Church, NE

Morning Prayer

Jesus, may all young people travel safely today.

—Amanda, Immaculate Conception Church, IA

Midday Prayer

Lord, bless all those who are in need of prayer, even when they are afraid to ask.

—Meghan, Our Lady of Peace Church, NJ

Evening Prayer

Dear God, please grant me the strength and knowledge to know what is right in troubling times.

—Ben, Saint Apollinaris High School, CA

Morning Prayer

Lord, help us to remember that you are always with us.

—Neil, Saint Michael Church, IL

Midday Prayer

God, please bless all young people to have the courage to share their faith.

—Ashley, Nativity Church, IN

Evening Prayer

Dear God, thank you for my gifts and talents and help me to use them to honor your name.

—Timothy, Saint Mary Church, MN

Morning Prayer

Help us to remember that you, God, created us to love one another and treat one another with dignity.

—Willis, DeLaSalle High School, MN

Midday Prayer

Thank you, Lord, for helping me to enjoy living again.

—Mariel, Saint Mary Church, MI

Evening Prayer

God, please help me to treat everyone with kindness and respect.

—Tommy, Sacred Heart High School, OH

Morning Prayer

With courage and power, allow me, Lord, to be reckless in carrying out your will.

—Carlee, Saint Mary of the Springs Church, AR

Midday Prayer

Dear God, I thank you for my friends, who care for me, laugh with me, are there for me, and love me. Please bless them with love and care.

—Lola, Saint Elizabeth of Hungary
High School, TX

Evening Prayer

Help us to stay strong and never give up, for you, God, are always with us.

—Rebecca, John Carroll High School, FL

Morning Prayer

Lord, let us better the lives of the people around us, through proclaiming your Word.

—Ruairi, Marist College Canberra, Australia

Midday Prayer

For those who are suffering, I pray.

—Jack, DeLaSalle High School, MN

Evening Prayer

Let me accept others the way you accept me, O Lord.

—Maleah, Pacelli High School, WI

Morning Prayer

Thank you, God, for the gift of life. I am made in your image, and that is good!

—Allison, Cotter High School, MN

Midday Prayer

For all those who, by the pressure of society, find it diffikult to be true to themselves and their gender identity, I pray.

—Emily, Providence High School, IN

Evening Prayer

God, please keep me strong through difficult times.

—Hannah, Dow High School, MI

Morning Prayer

Lord, let us remember that hope is always with us, as are you.

—Zachary, Meadville Area Catholic
Youth Ministry, PA

Midday Prayer

I pray that all people (including myself) learn to treat one another with equal respect.

—Alex, Sacred Heart of Jesus Church, OH

Evening Prayer

Lord, give me the courage to stand for my faith each day.

—Piers, Saint Philip Neri Church, OK

Morning Prayer

Gracious Lord, let me be mindful today that you are with me in all my trials as well as my successes.

—Irma, Prince of Peace Church, NM

Midday Prayer

I pray for anyone suffering or in pain; may they find comfort in you, God.

—Michael, Sacred Heart of Jesus Church, OH

Evening Prayer

Lord, may I find the good in others and focus on that.

—Charles, Providence High School, IN

Morning Prayer

Dear Lord, please help me to see every person
as a child of God, and help me to treat everyone
with the respect they deserve.

—Brennan, Cotter High School, MN

Midday Prayer

For those who are close to death, I pray.

—Alexandra, Saint Francis Borgia Regional
High School, MO

Evening Prayer

My God, help me to stay committed to you
always.

—Molly, Providence High School, IN

Morning Prayer

Lord, help me to keep my faith, trust, and hope in you throughout my life and especially during the most difficult times.

—Morgan, Saint Francis Borgia Regional
High School, MO

Midday Prayer

I pray for the quiet ones whose voices are never heard; may they realize that God is listening.

—Felecia, DeLaSalle High School, MN

Evening Prayer

God, thank you for all the things you have done for me today. I may not understand why you did them, but I thank you for them all.

—Natalie, Saint Elizabeth Church, MA

Morning Prayer

Dear God, make us people of faith, as we live every day for your Son, Jesus Christ. Though we face obstacles that threaten our belief, may we fall at your feet.

—Alden, Saint Matthew Church, TN

Midday Prayer

For those struggling with no self-confidence and depression, I pray.

—Harley, Mount Carmel High School, IL

Evening Prayer

I pray for peace and happiness.

—Emily, Guardian Angel Central High School, NE

Morning Prayer

Help us to remember that we are never alone; you are always there, no matter what.

—Joy, Delone High School, PA

Midday Prayer

Heavenly God, I pray for all those overseas fighting for our country.

—Anonymous, Saint Catherine of Alexandria Church, MA

Evening Prayer

Lord, I don't know what my future holds, but I can't wait to spend it with you.

—Laura, Pacelli High School, WI

Morning Prayer

Jesus, help me to refocus my life around you.

—Rachel, Ascension Church, OH

Midday Prayer

Please help all those in relationships to be able to communicate with each other well.

—Elsa, Providence High School, IN

Evening Prayer

Lord, there are many different paths in front of me. Help me to pick the right one.

—Aaron, Holy Family Church, MO

Morning Prayer

Teach me, Lord, to be brave when I need to be, and to find comfort in the fact that it's okay to be afraid.

—Kathryn, Delone High School, PA

Midday Prayer

I pray to you, Lord, for all of those struggling with future goals.

—Mina, Mother of Sorrows Church, PA

Evening Prayer

Dear Jesus, take me and make me the person you want me to be.

—Therese, Saint John High School, KS

Morning Prayer

I pray to you, Lord, that starting today, my life will change.

—Xiomara, Saint Maria Goretti Church, PA

Midday Prayer

Heavenly God, thank you for the gift of your love. Keep me pure in heart as I wait for my future spouse.

—Kaitlyn, Our Lady of Peace Church, NJ

Evening Prayer

God, give me the ability to remember what I've been taught today and apply it tomorrow.

—Doug, Our Lady of Lourdes Church, MO

Morning Prayer

God, please help me to develop healthy relationships.

—Casey, Cotter High School, MN

Midday Prayer

For all those who are overworked, I pray.

—Mikayla, Good Shepherd Church, PA

Evening Prayer

Lord, give me the strength to always put your will before mine.

—Danielle, Bishop Grimes High School, NY

Morning Prayer

Thank you, Lord, for everything you do for me, and help me to be more grateful and not take anything for granted.

—Morgan, Cotter High School, MN

Midday Prayer

I pray for all those who feel alone, that they remember God is there.

—Gabrielle, DeLaSalle High School, MN

Evening Prayer

Lord, help us, even during the darkest night, to see the light of day, and to remember that you are helping us every step of our journey.

—Sarah, Delone High School, PA

Morning Prayer

God, help me with all of my everyday needs and give me strength to face all my challenges.

—Kevin, Cotter High School, MN

Midday Prayer

I pray for those who are heartbroken, to not feel sadness but happiness.

—Jenna, Saint Elizabeth of Hungary
High School, TX

Evening Prayer

Dear God, help me to remember I can do all things through you.

—Katie, Saint Barnabas Church, OH

Morning Prayer

Cleanse me of anything that breaks your heart, O God.

—Gwendolyn, Providence High School, IN

Midday Prayer

Lord, I pray for anyone who is being bullied; may they have the courage to speak up for themselves.

—Sarah, Good Shepherd Church, VA

Evening Prayer

Thank you, God, for everything you've done for me. I really appreciate it, and I love everything I have.

—Cedric, Cotter High School, MN

Morning Prayer

Lord, be my guide when I am lost, and show me the path to you.

—Tyler, Saint Francis Borgia Regional
High School, MO

Midday Prayer

I pray for all soldiers overseas and their safe return home.

—Kelsey, Sacred Heart Church, IN

Evening Prayer

Use me, Lord, so others see your light through me.

—Allie, Saint Francis Borgia Regional
High School, MO

Morning Prayer

God, help us to love our enemies as Jesus did.

—Lauren, Saint Francis of Assisi Church, IA

Midday Prayer

I pray for all youth to have the courage to live out a pure, chaste, and virtuous life.

—Sarah, Our Lady of Peace Church, NJ

Evening Prayer

Lord, I pray for those who haven't found your light yet.

—Emily, Saint James Church, KY

Morning Prayer

I know that troubles come and go, but you, Lord, are always near. When we are in need, help us to turn to you.

—Jillian, Our Lady of Mercy Church, IL

Midday Prayer

I pray that all teens will always remember that they are beautiful and that God made them each special.

—Elena, Saint Patrick Church

Evening Prayer

Lord, help us to remember that Jesus loves us no matter what we are facing.

—Evan, Saint Peter Church, TX

Morning Prayer

Fill our hearts with hope, God.

—Joseph, Saint Elizabeth Ann Seton
Church, FL

Midday Prayer

I pray that Pope Francis continues to inspire all followers of Christ.

—Brenden, Sacred Heart Church, OH

Evening Prayer

Lord, thank you for your continued grace and support every day of my life. Help me to live in your light.

—Alex, Cotter High School, MN

Morning Prayer

Help us, Lord, to remember that we are stronger than we think.

—Connor, Saint Michael Church, IL

Midday Prayer

God, please be with all those who are homeless, living on the streets with no family to go to for help.

—Brady, La Salle High School, OH

Evening Prayer

Jesus, I place all my trust in you because I want to love you. Please let others do the same and follow through with their actions so that we can all be in Heaven together one day.

—Felipe, Xavier High School, NY

Morning Prayer

Help me to realize that all people have a place in this world.

—Erin, Saint Mary Church, ND

Midday Prayer

Dear God, please help me to get good grades.

—Jeremy, Cotter High School, MN

Evening Prayer

Thank you, Lord, for your unlimited goodness and mercy. Continue to guide us toward your plan.

—Alyson, Saint Elizabeth of Hungary
High School, TX

Morning Prayer

Heal me, O God. I believe in you.

—Melissa, Ascension Church, ND

Midday Prayer

I pray for those who are hurt, lonely, depressed, or beaten down, that they find faith in God and reach happiness.

—Rehgan, Saint Francis Borgia Regional High School, MO

Evening Prayer

God, thanks for being with me.

—Justin, Houma-Thibodaux, LA

Morning Prayer

Lord, remind us that when nothing goes right, don't go left, go to God.

—Jessica, Nativity Church, IN

Midday Prayer

God, please guide all women considering abortion to choose life.

—Payton, Sacred Heart of Jesus Church, OH

Evening Prayer

Help to guide me, Lord, onto the right path when I stray, and help me to grow in my faith.

—Alex, Cotter High School, MN

Morning Prayer

Lord, may you always be in my thoughts, in my words, and in my actions.

—Sarah, Good Shepherd Church, VA

Midday Prayer

I offer to you, God, my prayer for friends facing difficult choices.

—Leah, Saint Bernard Church, KY

Evening Prayer

May all those who have turned from you, Lord, find their way back.

—Kathryn, Saint Ann Church, IN

Morning Prayer

Lord, I believe. Help me in my disbelief (Mark 9:24).

—Joey, Saint Brigid of Kildare Church, MI

Midday Prayer

I pray for all the homeless and hungry; may God bless them with love and happiness.

—Anonymous, Saint Catherine of Alexandria Church, MA

Evening Prayer

Dear Lord, help me to recognize what is best for me.

—Amelie, Saint Elizabeth Ann Seton Church, TX

Morning Prayer

God, help me to always remember that despite all the tweets, texts, and e-mails, the best way to get in touch with oneself is through prayer.

—Oyeyemi, Saint Mary Academy, RI

Midday Prayer

I pray for all parents who have cancer.

—Clare, Saint Therese High School, MN

Evening Prayer

Father, enlighten our hearts and minds that we may be a sacrament to others and a light to the world.

—Rod, Saint Christopher Church, CA

Morning Prayer

Lord, teach me the way to strive for success and never lose faith in myself.

—Todd, Saint Francis Borgia Regional High School, MO

Midday Prayer

I pray for all grandparents who are struggling with their health.

—Tori, DeLaSalle High School, MN

Evening Prayer

May you, God, shine your light down on my life.

—Joe, Cotter High School, MN

Morning Prayer

God, give strength and courage to those
struggling under the weight of their own cross.

—Ezriel, Paramus High School, NJ

Midday Prayer

I pray for all pets. Thank you for the love they offer
us.

—Charles, Providence High School, IN

Evening Prayer

God, remind me that I have not only you but also
my family to support me in rough times.

—Amelia, Providence High School, IN

Morning Prayer

Thank you, Jesus Christ, for giving me my family.

—Emily, Notre Dame-Cathedral Latin
High School, OH

Midday Prayer

I pray that new babies grow up to be strong,
confident individuals with right values in life.

—Emma, Saint Francis Borgia Regional
High School, MO

Evening Prayer

God, please help me to say the right things even
when I'm angry.

—Julia, Christ the Redeemer Church, MI

Morning Prayer

For anyone who needs an increase in faith, I pray today.

—Nicole, Bishop Brossart High School, KY

Midday Prayer

I pray for any teens who have lost their father, that they will live life to the fullest, lives their dad would be proud of.

—Cynthia, Saint Michael Church, NY

Evening Prayer

Lord, help me to remember that you are a great God.

—Katie, Cotter High School, MN

Morning Prayer

In your loving presence, God, may we have
patience and forgiveness for those who do wrong
against us.

—Abel, DeLaSalle High School, MN

Midday Prayer

Lord, I pray for everyone affected by autism.

—Hunter, John Carroll High School, FL

Evening Prayer

Help me to put you, God, above less important
things in my life.

—Anonymous, MO

Morning Prayer

Help us to remember that life goes on, so we
should try to enjoy the beauty of it while we can.

—Austin, Pacelli High School, WI

Midday Prayer

I pray for everyone in the world.

—Dylan, La Salle High School, OH

Evening Prayer

Dear God, please help my friends to find your
light and begin to worship you.

—Samantha, Holy Spirit Church, IN

Morning Prayer

Lord, help all young people to stay true to themselves despite what others think.

—Kaitlyn, Providence High School, IN

Midday Prayer

God, help us to reach out to those considered outcasts.

—Mary, MO

Evening Prayer

Keep your watchful eyes, Lord, on those who are struggling with great decisions. May you strengthen them.

—Samantha, Harrah High School, OK

Morning Prayer

Help me to trust in you, God, and to become all
that I can be through you.

—Kayley, Our Lady of Angels Church, MN

Midday Prayer

I pray today, for my family and friends.

—Romina, Saint Francis Xavier Church, GA

Evening Prayer

Lord, as I commit myself to you, protect me and
allow me to keep my morals.

—Bryce, Saint Barnabas Church, IN

Morning Prayer

Help me to make my faith stronger, O Lord.

—Nick, Saint Mary Church, MO

Midday Prayer

Please help me to stay true to my friends and be with them in their time of need.

—Abby, Saint Jude Church, IN

Evening Prayer

I pray for all those who are embarking on a new journey in their lives. May they have strength to let go of everything they know now and have the courage to embrace God's new plan for them.

—Lizzy, DeLaSalle High School, MN

Morning Prayer

Lord, give me the strength to live like a Christian, even when it's not easy.

—Lauren, Saint Joan of Arc Church, IN

Midday Prayer

I pray for the homeless.

—Kris, Sacred Heart Church, KS

Evening Prayer

Dear God, please help me to bring those turning away from you back under your wing.

—Mattie-Catherine, Our Lady of the Lakes Church, IN

Morning Prayer

Lord, give me the courage to reach out and radiate your divine love.

—Jen, MT

Midday Prayer

Lord, be with those who are trying to recover from typhoons and other natural disasters.

—Michelle, Good Shepherd Church, CA

Evening Prayer

Thank you, Lord, for everything you have done and will do in my life and for the people who are close to me.

—Dalton, Saint Katherine Drexel Church, MN

Morning Prayer

God, you are my sun and my moon. Thank you.

—Kaycee, Saint Anne Church, ND

Midday Prayer

I pray for all of those struggling with self-esteem; may they find the strength to be confident and love themselves.

—Kaitlyn, Saint Anthony Church, IN

Evening Prayer

God, give me the power to protect those I care about.

—Kevin, Saint Joseph Church, MD

Morning Prayer

Dear God, allow everyone to be the best person they can be today.

—David, Saint William Church, MD

Midday Prayer

I pray for the ones who have lost their view of faith; may they find God's light again.

—Madison, Immaculate Conception Church, NY

Evening Prayer

I pray that God opens my heart to new experiences.

—Maura, Diocese of Helena, MT

Morning Prayer

Lord, please help my family to strive in your name.

—Angelina, Mother Cabrini Church, TX

Midday Prayer

Dear God, please help me to get through this year of school.

—Allison, Saint Francis Borgia Regional
High School, MO

Evening Prayer

I pray that you, God, bless all those I've been blessed to share today with.

—Sam, Providence High School, IN

Morning Prayer

God, help me to make the most of today.

—John, Saint Apollinaris High School, CA

Midday Prayer

I pray that there is a cure to cancer so no more families have to experience suffering and loss.

—Savannah, Diocese of Helena, MT

Evening Prayer

I pray that you, Lord, will give me the strength to spread Jesus' love to everyone I know even if I do not like them or if they are not nice to me.

—Anella, Redwood Valley High School, MN

Morning Prayer

Dear Lord, please help me to have not only the acceptance of others but also that of myself.

—Katlyn, Saint Mary Church, MO

Midday Prayer

Please help all people who are being bullied on a regular basis, at school or at home, to find peace with God.

—Austin, Saint Francis Borgia Regional High School, MO

Evening Prayer

Thank you for the support of my friends who are loyal to me and help me in hard times.

—Kyle, Saint Catherine of Alexandria Church, MA

Morning Prayer

Dear Lord, please give me the strength to face the hardships in life..

—Veronica, Sacred Heart Church, MD

Midday Prayer

I pray for starving children and adults.

—Eddie, All Saints Church, KS

Evening Prayer

God, give me the virtues that I need to win the race.

—Haylee, Oldenburg Academy, IN

Morning Prayer

Dear God, please give me the strength each day to love others.

—Nick, Saint Michael Church, OH

Midday Prayer

I pray that the homeless find shelter and the hungry find food.

—Rose, Saint Francis Xavier Church, KS

Evening Prayer

God, I ask that your peace surpasses all my fears and anxieties so that I may live joyfully for your glory.

—Quinn, Seton High School, OH

Morning Prayer

Lord, help me to be who I am.

—Stephanie, Saint Cecilia Church, MN

Midday Prayer

I pray for those who need mercy.

—Anna, Holy Family Church, FL

Evening Prayer

Lord, I am not afraid, for you are always with me.

—Kate, Saint Mary Church, IN

Morning Prayer

Lord, teach me to love as selflessly as you have loved me.

—Jordan, Saint Mary Help of Christians Church, SC

Midday Prayer

Virgen de Guadalupe te ruego que cuidas y ayudas a la gente en los Phillipenos. Ellos esten en ruinas por la violencia y el estado de su pais. Te lo pido en el nombre de nuestro señor. Amen.

—Gaby, Saint Edward Church, OR

Evening Prayer

Thank you, Father, for all of the wonderful activities, friends, and families you have given us.

—Nathan, Saint Bernadette Church, KY

Morning Prayer

Dear God, please help me to be less selfish.

—Jackie, Saint Francis Church, OH

Midday Prayer

I pray for mothers everywhere, that they will choose life and enjoy the absolute gift and miracle of a child.

—Lily, Saint Mary Academy, OR

Evening Prayer

Lord, may this world have peace.

—Blair, Saint Louis Church, KS

Morning Prayer

God, please be with me today.

—Katie, Sacred Heart Church, MN

Midday Prayer

Lord, I pray that all people can become more accepting of Catholics and others whose faith is different from theirs.

—Madeline, Notre Dame High School, IA

Evening Prayer

Please help all people to be strong and to thank you for all gifts.

—Mary, Saint Edward Church, OR

Morning Prayer

Lord, take my heart into your hands and guide my steps today.

—Miranda, Saint Francis of Assisi Church, CO

Midday Prayer

I pray for all people to treat each other fairly.

—Nicholas, Our Lady of Providence Church, IN

Evening Prayer

Please give me the strength to carry on through times of hurtfulness.

—Emily, Saint Mary's Springs Academy, WI

Morning Prayer

For the strength to overcome all of life's challenges, hear me, Lord.

—Toystan, Ascension Church, ND

Midday Prayer

I pray for those who suffer secretly with the pain of torture and abuse. Give them courage and hope, Lord, to stand up to their abusers.

—Aaron, Saint Francis Borgia Regional High School, MO

Evening Prayer

God, help all of my relationships to stay Christ-centered.

—Noah, Saint Sebastian Church, PA

Morning Prayer

Lord, help me to evangelize and live up to the Christian standards.

—Ayana, Saint Mary Margaret Church, IL

Midday Prayer

I pray for everyone taking tests today.

—Beth, Cotter High School, MN

Evening Prayer

Dear God, lead me through the narrow path.

—Matt, Cotter High School, MN

Morning Prayer

Today is a new day, Lord. Help me to make the best of it.

—Madison, Saint Joan of Arc Church, IN

Midday Prayer

I pray for those who are lost and are yearning to be found by Jesus Christ.

—Peter, Holy Cross Church, IL

Evening Prayer

Let us remember that God is God.

—Clara, Good Shepherd Church, KS

Morning Prayer

Lord, give me the courage to stand up for those who can't stand up for themselves.

—Joe, Thomas More Prep High School, KS

Midday Prayer

I pray today for you, God, to look down on all of those getting bullied and help them through their hard times, and to keep them safe.

—Zach, Saint Francis Borgia Regional
High School, MO

Evening Prayer

Dear God, help me to stay strong in my faith.

—Anonymous

Morning Prayer

Lord, help me to be the daughter you look down on and say, "That's my girl."

—Grace, Christ the King Church, GA

Midday Prayer

Dear God, please help everyone with their troubles and help everyone to succeed.

—Andy, Cotter High School, MN

Evening Prayer

I pray that we will be blessed with the ability to help one another strive in daily life.

—Jill, Saint Francis Borgia Regional High School, MO

Morning Prayer

Dear Lord, please help me to overcome the pressure of society and its "perfect" image of a person.

—Josie, Saint Jude Church, IN

Midday Prayer

I pray for all those who feel like they don't belong.

—Abby, Nativity Church, IN

Evening Prayer

I ask you, O God, for a pure, wholesome relationship.

—Sarah, Good Shepherd Church, VA

Morning Prayer

God, grant me the strength to remember you in my trials and the ability to stand up to those trials.

—Scott, Providence High School, IN

Midday Prayer

I pray for all those struggling with their faith.

—Calvin, Saint Francis Borgia Regional
High School, MO

Evening Prayer

Help us to remember that you, God, have a plan for each of us and that you have our best interests in mind.

—Sophia, Saint Elizabeth of Hungary
High School, TX

Morning Prayer

Jesus, please help us to fill our hearts with fire so that we can change the world.

—Brian, Archbishop O'Hara High School, MO

Midday Prayer

Lord, when I'm in need, remind me that Jesus is there.

—Paul, Christ the King Church, IN

Evening Prayer

Dear Mother Mary, pray for those of us who are in despair, and give us joy.

—Yessenia, Saint John High School, KS

Morning Prayer

Jesus, please help me to be the person you made me to be, want me to be, and know I can be.

—Emily, Saint Joan of Arc Church, IN

Midday Prayer

I pray that my future spouse loves the Lord so much.

—Lauretta, North Olmsted High School, OH

Evening Prayer

Help me, God, to love others as you have loved me.

—Katie, Our Lady of the Lakes Church, IN

Morning Prayer

Dear heavenly Father, please give me the strength and potential I need to carry on through this day.

—Lisette, Saint Elizabeth of Hungary
High School, TX

Midday Prayer

I pray for those who have left the path God has chosen for them.

—Lauren, Saint Joseph Church, KS

Evening Prayer

God, take the fear away from me, for fear is only temporary, but you are forever.

—Taylor, Providence High School, IN

Morning Prayer

Lord, please watch over me; Jesus, please lead the way; Holy Spirit, help me to follow.

—George, Saint Aloysius Church, CT

Midday Prayer

God, give all who are sick strength and faith to pull them through.

—Dan, DeLaSalle High School, MN

Evening Prayer

I pray that my faith in you, God, will continue to grow as I get older.

—Gabrielle, Saint Elizabeth of Hungary High School, TX

Morning Prayer

Lord, please protect my family and friends,and show me the way to be a good steward.

—Jorge, Bishop Moore High School, FL

Midday Prayer

That all souls will one day make it to Heaven, I pray.

—Ashley, Providence High School, IN

Evening Prayer

I pray that all people in our world can overcome their barriers, and we can exist together as one in our faith in Christ.

—Remington, Notre Dame Cathedral
High School, OH

Morning Prayer

Oh Lord, may we recognize your glory in our daily lives as we continue to live in your glorious creation.

—Peter, Cotter High School, MN

Midday Prayer

Lord, my prayer is for all those who have internal struggles.

—Whitney, Saint Joseph Church, KS

Evening Prayer

I pray for friends. I pray for family. I pray for life.

—Anonymous, Saint Catherine of Alexandria Church, MA

Morning Prayer

Dear heavenly Father, thank you for all the wonderful things you give me every day, including friends, family, life, and your unconditional love.

—Diamond, DeLaSalle High School, MN

Midday Prayer

I pray for the sick, that they may have faith in God no matter what.

—Natalie, Saint Elizabeth of Hungary High School, TX

Evening Prayer

Oh Lord, at the times I am filled with grief and sorrow, provide me with the love, support, and strength I need to go on.

—Amy, Mercy High School, MI

Morning Prayer

I pray for the courage to get through the day with a positive attitude.

—Christy, Terrebonne High School, LA

Midday Prayer

Dear Lord, help others to make right decisions and to be themselves no matter what happens in their lives. Show them that you are always by their side.

—Taylor, Saint Francis Borgia Regional High School, MO

Evening Prayer

O God, may I never put the key to my success in someone else's pocket.

—Mary, DeLaSalle High School, MN

Morning Prayer

Dear God, the world gives us many reasons to be
daunted, but with your help I'll show the world I
have twice the number of reasons to be fearless.

—Anna Marie, Delone High School, PA

Midday Prayer

Lord, help all those on the wrong path.

—Aleishka, Saint Maria Goretti Church, PA

Evening Prayer

Lord, I offer this prayer for all family members
suffering from physical pain.

—Rachel, Immaculate Conception
High School, IA

Morning Prayer

God, help me not to be afraid to tell people how
I feel.

—Lilly, Providence High School, IN

Midday Prayer

Lord, please be with everyone who doesn't have a
loving family.

—Brice, West Hancock High School, IA

Evening Prayer

Lord, help us to remember that fear is nothing but
a thought.

—Josh, Cotter High School, MN

Morning Prayer

Jesus, help me to remember to keep my family close and God closer.

—Dalton, Providence High School, IN

Midday Prayer

I pray for people to conquer their fears.

—Jared, Saint Elizabeth of Hungary
High School, TX

Evening Prayer

Lord, help all to let go and let God.

—Catherine, Saint Catherine Church, MA

Morning Prayer

God, help me to remember that in all my struggles
I must be still and know that you are God.

—Katie, Saint Robert Church, MI

Midday Prayer

I pray that struggling families get along better and
do not take each other for granted.

—Anonymous, Father Ryan High School, TN

Evening Prayer

Lord, help me when my faith is most shaken.

—Ashley, Saint Mary Church, FL

Morning Prayer

Dear Lord, please hear my thoughts of worry, and give me strength to overcome my daily fears.

—Ann, Blessed Trinity Church, MI

Midday Prayer

I pray for the guidance in leadership of all sports teams.

—Jared, Good Shepherd Church, PA

Evening Prayer

God, you are the light of the world and the light of my life. I praise you.

—Jacob, Cotter High School, MN

Morning Prayer

Father, with your aid and constant guidance, I pray that your purpose for me is fulfilled. Amen.

—Cheri, Saint Rita Church, MI

Midday Prayer

I pray, God, for teens who are caught between two contrasting interests.

—Katie, Holy Family Church, IA

Evening Prayer

Lord, help us to have no fear, Jesus is here.

—Jack, Saint Edward Church, IN

Morning Prayer

Lord, be with me.

—Mikey, Saint Michael Church, IL

Midday Prayer

I pray, God, for those who are afraid to follow their dreams.

—Nathan, MN

Evening Prayer

Lord, keep my fears at bay when I slumber.

—Jaylee, Saint John the Baptist Church, IA

Morning Prayer

Please, God, remove fear and anxiety from my heart so that I may be able to focus on your Word.

—Emily, Saint Mary of the Assumption Church, NY

Midday Prayer

My prayer is for everyone at war.

—Maggie, City High School, IA

Evening Prayer

Lord, I do not always fit in; however, when I think of you, I can be myself to the tiniest detail, without feeling pressured to be like someone else. Thank you.

—Elizabeth, Cotter High School, MN

Morning Prayer

Dear God, help all of us to overcome our past and to look forward to the future.

—Matthew, Mount Carmel High School, NJ

Midday Prayer

I pray for all grandparents fighting cancer.

—Sierra, Mercy Academy, KY

Evening Prayer

Grant me the grace, Lord, to love with no fear.

—Clare, Saint Teresa Academy, MO

Morning Prayer

Dear Lord, help me to always look out for my friends and to help them when they are in need. Help us all to walk in your footsteps, which lead us to eternal life.

—Megan, Bishop Grimes High School, NY

Midday Prayer

I pray for all teens dealing with divorce.

—Elise, Walsh Jesuit High School, OH

Evening Prayer

Thank you, God, for all that you have given me.

—Bailey, Cotter High School, MN

Morning Prayer

Lord, please help me to remember that everyone has a complicated and compelling story and should be treated with respect, patience, and understanding.

—Clara, Saint Francis Borgia Regional High School, MO

Midday Prayer

Throughout the world many children are being used as child soldiers. Please help them, O God.

—Regdirb, Marist College Canberra, Australia

Evening Prayer

Lord, for my self-improvement and for that of others, I pray.

—Jung Suk, Cotter High School, MN

Morning Prayer

I pray for the courage to proclaim my love for you, God, no matter who is listening.

—Katie, Saint Columban College, Australia

Midday Prayer

Dear God, keep my peers safe as they move through life.

—Taylor, Saint Peter Church, MO

Evening Prayer

Cast down your Spirit, into my heart, mind, and body, O Lord.

—Zachary, Chaminade Julienne
High School, OH

Morning Prayer

Lord, I'm grateful for my family and friends each and every day. Thank you.

—Katie, Saint Francis Borgia Regional
High School, MO

Midday Prayer

I pray for those suffering through civil war in Africa.

—Jason, Cotter High School, MN

Evening Prayer

Holy Spirit, help me to be the person God wants me to be.

—Kendall, Delone High School, PA

Morning Prayer

Dear God, please help me to always keep faith in your guidance.

—Allison, Saint Francis Borgia Regional
High School, MO

Midday Prayer

For the people who need hope in their lives, that you, God, will show them the way, I pray.

—Elizabeth, Saint Elizabeth of Hungary
High School, TX

Evening Prayer

I thank you, Lord, for all you do for us. You help us to gain friends and make long-lasting friendships.

—Ryan, Cotter High School, MN

Morning Prayer

Come, brother and sisters, let us praise and give thanks to the Lord for his glorious creation.

—Kristen, Delone High School, PA

Midday Prayer

I pray that one day everyone who has lost hope finds it in Christ.

—Allie, Saint Michael Church, PA

Evening Prayer

I thank you, God, for what you have given to me, and I pray for those who don't have anyone to pray for them.

—Allie, Nerinx Hall High School, MO

Morning Prayer

God, help us to be the greatest students by learning from you, the greatest teacher.

—Bowen, Marist College Canberra, Australia

Midday Prayer

My prayer is for those in need.

—Javan, DeLaSalle High School, MN

Evening Prayer

Let me be myself, Lord, and in doing so, may I be happy.

—Tori, Nerinx Hall High School, MO

Morning Prayer

This morning, Lord, help me to "Do it for Jesus!"

—Luke, Saint Patrick Church, IA

Midday Prayer

May the people in the Middle East feel your love, O God.

—Gina, Sacred Heart of Jesus Church, OH

Evening Prayer

Lord, please help me to find joy and happiness in the hardest times.

—Kristina, Marquette High School, IA

Morning Prayer

Lord, may you give us the grace to accept,
respect, and love ourselves.

—Christina, DeLaSalle High School, MN

Midday Prayer

Jesus, please grant serenity and level-headedness
to those who need it.

—Marcus, Saint Francis Borgia Regional
High School, MO

Evening Prayer

Lord, please give me the strength to see my trials
as a part of your grand design, as you are helping
me to be the best person I am called to be.

—Haley, Blanchet Catholic High School, OR

Morning Prayer

When I am feeling down, Lord, please help me to stay positive and persevere through the day.

—Lauren, DeLaSalle High School, MN

Midday Prayer

I pray for my parents, O God.

—Ruohong, Cotter High School, MN

Evening Prayer

I pray that we love our neighbors like Christ did, because life as a teenager would be a lot easier if we were nice to one another.

—Hannah, Saint Monica Church, IN

Morning Prayer

God, teach me to be loyal and friendly to everyone in my life.

—Kelli, Saint Francis Borgia Regional High School, MO

Midday Prayer

Please, Lord, give me the strength to complete all my tests to my best ability.

—Rebecca, Providence High School, IN

Evening Prayer

We all have more than we think. We give you thanks, God.

—Abby, Saint Joseph of Spreckels Church, CA

Morning Prayer

Lord, apart from you I can do nothing. I praise you.

—Pamela, Saint Mary Catholic School, MD

Midday Prayer

Just as you gave Archbishop Oscar Romero a voice for the voiceless, Lord, give a voice to all those who don't have one.

—Connor, DeLaSalle High School, MN

Evening Prayer

Dear God, help me to find your way.

—Sean, Saint Bartholomew Church, IN

Morning Prayer

I pray for the strength to be myself and keep my values.

—Emma, Saint Anthony Church, IN

Midday Prayer

Lord, please help teens as they make future decisions for college and jobs.

—Bailey, Saint Joseph Church, IN

Evening Prayer

God, give me a future that is as bright as the sun.

—Jared, Saint Patrick Church, NE

Morning Prayer

Dear God, please don't let fear rule my life; help me to let you take control.

—Megan, Incarnation Church, OH

Midday Prayer

I pray to you, Lord, that people learn to love one another and help the needy.

—Gage, Saint Michael Church, MI

Evening Prayer

Thank you, God, for love in life, friendship, dating, and marriage.

—Kevin, Saint Catherine of
Alexandria Church, MA

Morning Prayer

I thank you, God, for the gift of this day and all it will bring.

—Mary, Incarnation Church, OH

Midday Prayer

For all who are struggling with their senior year of school, I pray, O God.

—Kristina, Holy Trinity Church, MD

Evening Prayer

Lord, please give me the strength to always do what is right.

—Emily, Saint Mary Church, MI

Morning Prayer

Lord, I ask for the courage to live out my day as a good and holy Catholic.

—Maddie, Incarnation Church, OH

Midday Prayer

I offer this prayer for those who are unaware of God's love.

—Mary, Saint Mary High School, MI

Evening Prayer

To those who we may hurt, help us, Lord, to say, "I love you, I'm sorry, please forgive me, and thank you."

—Dan, Saint Paul Church, NJ

Morning Prayer

For the courage to be true to ourselves and our
faith in every situation, I pray.

—Anna, Batesville High School, IN

Midday Prayer

Lord, please be with every suicidal or bullied
person.

—Miranda, Bethlehem High School, KY

Evening Prayer

God, help me to share the faith with others and
spread your Word.

—Morgan, Annunciation Church, MO

Morning Prayer

God, give me an opportunity to shine.

—Shawna, Saint Catherine Church, MN

Midday Prayer

I pray for all teens that you, Lord, may guide them today and all days.

—Jessica, Bishop Ward High School, KS

Evening Prayer

Lord, may all understand that there is always hope.

—Jacob, Saint Martha Church, KY

Morning Prayer

Dear Lord, help me to grow closer to you and get
to know you more each and every day.

—Ashley, Saint Ignatius Church, MD

Midday Prayer

Jesus, please help all those who are suffering.
May they find strength in you.

—Jordyn, Bishop Browart High School, KY

Evening Prayer

In the darkest cave, you are the light that shines. I
praise you, God.

—Daniel, Trinity Church, KY

Morning Prayer

Dear Lord, please give me strength to get through times of hardship.

—Jennifer, Saint Ann Church, MN

Midday Prayer

I pray for all of those who have taken their lives due to bullying.

—Rachel, Saint Paul the Apostle Church, OH

Evening Prayer

Thank you, God, for the happiness I find in my friends, family, and community.

—Chris, Saint Catherine of Alexandria Church, MA

Morning Prayer

I pray that I might love others, as I have been loved by you, God . . . unconditionally.

—Raphael, Saint Joseph Church, KS

Midday Prayer

For all friendships, broken and failing, please, God, bring restoration to those who need it.

—Casten, Saint Patrick Church, NE

Evening Prayer

Lord, give me strength.

—Elizabeth, Saint Mary Help of Christians Church, SC

Morning Prayer

God, help me determine the difference between your true love and earthly lust.

—Bailey, Saint Francis of Assisi Church, IN

Midday Prayer

My prayer, Lord, is for those who are too afraid to ask for the help they need.

—Anne, Saint Paul Church, OH

Evening Prayer

For all the struggles I've been through, keep my faith strong, O God.

—Mark, Immaculate Conception Church, OH

Morning Prayer

Lord, help me to live my life to the fullest every day.

—Erica, Saint Cecilia Church, MN

Midday Prayer

I pray that bullying will stop.

—Cassidy, Saint Francis Church, KS

Evening Prayer

For the world to be on fire with the Holy Spirit, I pray to you, God.

—Heather, Holy Family Church, FL

Morning Prayer

God, whenever I struggle, please strengthen me, help me to get up when I fall. I love you.

—Johnny, Saint Mary Church, IN

Midday Prayer

I pray that my friends may profess their faith with passion.

—Boyd, Saint Aloysius Church, KS

Evening Prayer

Lord, I take a moment to offer a prayer for those with debilitating diseases.

—Angelo, Saint Anthony Church, WY

Morning Prayer

Help me to stay strong in my faith and to trust in you, God.

—Elizabeth, Saint Mary Church, KY

Midday Prayer

I pray for all of those who are bullied, especially those who have lost their lives because of it.

—Brooke, Saint Francis Borgia Regional High School, MO

Evening Prayer

Holy Spirit, hold my life in your hand and do with me what you will.

—Olivia, Saint Pius X Church, KY

Morning Prayer

Father God, through school and activities, please walk with me.

—Emily, Saint Patrick Church, WY

Midday Prayer

I pray for all military families in this world.

—Ellie, Holy Family Church, FL

Evening Prayer

Lord, help all people to have peace and love inside their hearts.

—Kaitlynn, Saint John Church, WY

Morning Prayer

May all students find happiness and love in our schools, I pray, O God.

—Marissa, Cal High School, CA

Midday Prayer

Dear Lord, give us motivation to stop procrastination across the nation.

—Danielle, Saint Patrick Church, IN

Evening Prayer

Thank you, God, for giving me the strength to overcome every struggle in my life.

—Ali, Saint Francis of Assissi Church, OH

Morning Prayer

Dear God, please help us to know that you are the Way.

—Libby, Saint Mary Church, KY

Midday Prayer

I pray for students going into nursing.

—Alyssa, Saint Anthony Church, WY

Evening Prayer

Lord, please give me a sign that I am loved.

—Megan, Saint Joseph Church, IN

Morning Prayer

Dear Lord, please calm my fears and increase my trust in you.

—Delaney, Sacred Heart Church, IN

Midday Prayer

I pray for those suffering from depression or self-harm. May they remember that they are precious in your eyes, God, and that you will never leave them alone in darkness.

—Christine, Saint Joan of Arc Church, IN

Evening Prayer

Help me to live in the light and love of you, Lord.

—Jared, Blessed Teresa of Calcutta Church, KY

Morning Prayer

Lord, give me strength to share my prayers with others.

—Shannon, Saint Patrick Church, WY

Midday Prayer

I offer my prayer for the safety of the unborn.

—Simon, Sacred Heart Church, MN

Evening Prayer

Dear God, please help me to remember what is right and to always know that it's important to love myself, more than trying to make someone else happy.

—Taylor, Saint Joseph Church, MI

Morning Prayer

May I always find trust in you Lord, our God.

—Molly, Saint Clara Church, MN

Midday Prayer

I pray that people with developmental disabilities be looked upon as one of the group rather than one that is different from the group.

—Rachael, Saratoga Central High School, NY

Evening Prayer

Make me a more perfect offering to your heart, God, for only that which comes from you is worthy of you.

—Clarke, Saint Joseph Church, KS

Morning Prayer

Lord, help those who need it most to stand up to their fears.

—Joe, Saint Francis Borgia Regional
High School, MO

Midday Prayer

For society and the strengthening of our faith, I pray.

—Anissa, TX

Evening Prayer

God, give me strength to be pure and wise in choosing a husband or wife.

—Elisabeth, Christ our Redeemer Church, FL

Morning Prayer

Lord, please help me to find a way to focus and to succeed.

—Sam, DeLaSalle High School, MN

Midday Prayer

I pray for young adults who make mistakes, that they may be forgiven and blessed.

—José, Saint Joseph Church, WI

Evening Prayer

O God Almighty, I offer you my heart and faith, and I thank you for all that you bless me with.

—Jasmine, Saint Patrick Church, WY

Morning Prayer

Lord, please strengthen the faith of those around me.

—Melanie, Incarnation High School, OH

Midday Prayer

Thank you, God, for helping me at school.

—Lacey, Epiphany of Our Lord Church, OK

Evening Prayer

Lord, help me to remember that you are my refuge.

—Noah, Providence High School, IN

Morning Prayer

God, please help us to remember that there is no need to fear, Jesus is here.

—Caroline, Saint Catherine Church, MA

Midday Prayer

I pray for those who have had their self-esteem taken; may they find someone to return it to them stronger than ever.

—Michael, Saint Francis Borgia Regional High School, MO

Evening Prayer

Lord, I thank you today and every day for the life you give me. I am also thankful for your heart-filled love that you spread over all.

—Emily, Cotter High School, MN

Morning Prayer

God, help those who are afraid to let go of their fears and let you take over.

—Josh, Saint Francis Borgia Regional High School, MO

Midday Prayer

God, please help all foster children in the world; may they find safe and loving homes to live out the rest of their lives.

—Matthew, Sacred Heart of Jesus Church, OH

Evening Prayer

Dear God, please keep the people I love healthy and safe.

—Lewis, Saint Francis Borgia Regional High School, MO

Morning Prayer

Lord, help me to be the person I am called to be.

—Dylan, Cotter High School, MN

Midday Prayer

I pray for peace on the streets of Chicago and all cities in our nation.

—Sierra, Incarnation High School, IL

Evening Prayer

Lord, help us to remember you will always be here, even through the darkest days.

—Kevin, Saint Michael Church, IL

Morning Prayer

Lord, help us to face our fears.

—Andrew, Cotter High School, MN

Midday Prayer

I pray for all recovering from cancer.

—Patrick, Putnam City North High School, OK

Evening Prayer

Dear God, thank you for having people who love and care for me in good and bad times.

—Joshua, La Salle High School, OH

Morning Prayer

God, please give us the courage to step away
from the crowd.

—Spencer, Saint Joseph Church, WI

Midday Prayer

I offer this prayer for friends who are struggling
with depression.

—Regan, Lourdes Catholic Church, IA

Evening Prayer

Lord, help me to not shy away from friends and
family in times of need.

—Joshua, Saint Francis Borgia Regional
High School, MO

Morning Prayer

Lord, I pray for the acceptance of all.

—Neal, Saint Francis Borgia Regional
High School, MO

Midday Prayer

I pray for the parents of children, that they are good examples through Christ.

—Isabella, Saint Joseph Church, KS

Evening Prayer

Thank you, God, for all the things you have given me and my family.

—Kaci, Saint Elizabeth of Hungary
High School, TX

Morning Prayer

Lord, please help me to value everything I have
and to not take anything for granted.

—Rachel, Bishop Grimes High School, NY

Midday Prayer

Today I pray for all those who have doubts in their
faith in Christ, and I pray that Jesus touches their
lives like he has mine.

—Anthony, Holy Angels Church, IN

Evening Prayer

God, O sweet God, please protect me from
violence.

—Sarah, Good Shepherd Church, VA

Morning Prayer

God, I pray for the friends we have and the friends we don't have.

—Lauren, Carroll High School, OH

Midday Prayer

I offer this prayer for those who feel a lack of love in their lives; may they be reminded of those who are there for them.

—Connor, DeLaSalle High School, MN

Evening Prayer

For all those suffering from the loss of a loved one, I pray, O God.

—Brianna, Saint Peter Church, WI

Morning Prayer

Lord, help me this day to remember you are always with me and will always love me no matter what I do.

—Cade, Cotter High School, MN

Midday Prayer

I pray that all souls will see God.

—Dustin, Diocese of Houma-Thibodaux, LA

Evening Prayer

God, help me to see through your eyes, to hear through your ears, and to love through your heart.

—Samantha, Notre Dame-Cathedral Latin High School, OH

Morning Prayer

I pray that I may become closer to you, God, through knowing you, loving you, and serving you.

—Clare, Bishop Watterson High School, OH

Midday Prayer

May all those who feel excluded know your presence, Lord.

—Mikey, Saint Barnabas Church, IN

Evening Prayer

Let me remember that the only way to true happiness is through you, O God.

—Mary, Roncalli High School, IN

Morning Prayer

Thank you, God, for loving and liking me.

—Alexandra, Saint Elizabeth Ann Seton
Church, MD

Midday Prayer

For my grandparents, I pray.

—David, Cotter High School, MN

Evening Prayer

I give you praise, Lord, for giving us friendships so
that we may have someone to lean on and have
fun with.

—Jason, DeLaSalle High School, MN

Morning Prayer

Help me, Lord, to surround myself with people that I love and people that love me.

—Troy, Pacelli High School, WI

Midday Prayer

I pray for the souls who are lost in pain, that they may find hope and healing through your Son, Jesus Christ.

—Sara, Our Lady of Providence Church, IN

Evening Prayer

God, please send good friends to me. May they be pure, kind, and generous. I do not ask for perfect friends, but if you would, please send me some caring, loving friends. I would be most grateful.

—Sarah, Good Shepherd Church, VA

Morning Prayer

Thank you, God, for blessing me with this wonderful life.

—Jared, Saint Francis Borgia Regional
High School, MO

Midday Prayer

I pray for all those who feel too weary to carry on in life. Be with them, Lord.

—Kaitlyn, Nerinx Hall High School, MO

Evening Prayer

Help me, O God, to walk with faith.

—Cede, Saint Patrick Church, IA

Morning Prayer

I pray for your Spirit, Lord, to shine through me
and give me the courage and strength to take on
this day.

—Zara, FL

Midday Prayer

Lord, I pray for everyone with cancer, especially
family members.

—Jared, Thomas More Prep High School, KS

Evening Prayer

Dear God, thank you for everything you do for
me.

—Allison, Cotter High School, MN

Morning Prayer

Help me to do all things through and for you,
God.

—Wesley, Saint Mary Church, KY

Midday Prayer

May all people respect and treat others the same.

—Rosa, Saint Gabriel Church, IN

Evening Prayer

Lord, I pray for a friend in Heaven.

—Chelsey, Our Lady of the Assumption Church, AR

Morning Prayer

Please give me hope, Lord, for I am without any at this time.

—Sarah, Good Shepherd Church, VA

Midday Prayer

I pray for safe travels across the world.

—Bailey, Saint John Church, KS

Evening Prayer

Lord, on my darkest day, lead me to your light.

—Emma, Sacred Heart Church, OH

Morning Prayer

Lord, give me strength and determination to follow my dreams when they may seem out of reach.

—Reid, DeLaSalle High School, MN

Midday Prayer

I pray for my grades and other schoolwork and projects.

—Israel, Saint Elizabeth of Hungary
High School, TX

Evening Prayer

Lord, you are so loving and caring. Send your grace to us in our everyday struggles.

—Maria, Christ the King Church, GA

Morning Prayer

Dear Lord, please help me to have a great day.

—Owen, Sacred Heart Church, OH

Midday Prayer

I pray for those who struggle to get through each day; may they find strength and hope within themselves.

—Natalia, Saint Benedict High School, IL

Evening Prayer

That we may persevere during the lowest of lows and stay humble during the highest of highs, I pray.

—Kevin, Saint Francis Borgia Regional High School, MO

Morning Prayer

God, lead me, guide me, and support me always.

—Anonymous

Midday Prayer

I offer my prayer for all those who have been affected by tornadoes and natural disasters; may we help them to get back on track with their lives.

—Jodi, Our Lady of Lourdes Church, IA

Evening Prayer

I praise you, O Lord, for you died for us on the cross.

—Jacob, Saint Casmir Church, MN

Morning Prayer

Lord God, I pray for your love and guidance to lead me through the insecurities and challenges I may face today.

—Julie, Our Lady of Providence Church, IN

Midday Prayer

My prayer is for all of the troops that are protecting our country, that they remain safe.

—Tyler, Marian High School, KS

Evening Prayer

Help the lonely, the broken, and the lost remember that they are loved by you, God.

—Megan, Saint Mary Church, IN

Morning Prayer

Please, Lord, let the world be a kind place, let justice show in the world, and let poverty end.

—Kaleb, Saint Mary Church, MN

Midday Prayer

For all those lost, I pray.

—Matthew, Father Ryan High School, TN

Evening Prayer

Dear God, thank you for this day today, and all the days to come; thank you for your wise advice and all the things you've done for me.

—Sami, Cotter High School, MN

Morning Prayer

Help me to realize that I don't need a romantic relationship to feel loved. All I need are friends, family, and you, God.

—Nichole, Bishop Grimes High School, NY

Midday Prayer

For those who are suffering and don't have anyone to pray for them, I offer this prayer.

—Meaghan, John Carroll High School, FL

Evening Prayer

May each day be better than the last, and thank you, Lord, for all that you have given me.

—Corey, Cotter High School, MN

Morning Prayer

God, help me to be forgiving.

—Tomas, DeLaSalle High School, MN

Midday Prayer

Lord, please help students who feel pressured in their studies to be able to relax and be confident in themselves.

—Jeremy, Saint Francis Borgia Regional High School, MO

Evening Prayer

My dearest Mother, open my heart and inflame within me your love so I may love your Son as you love him.

—Sarah, Holy Cross High School, NC

Morning Prayer

Jesus, help me through all the seemingly unimportant daily struggles.

—Max, Saint Francis Borgia Regional
High School, MO

Midday Prayer

I pray for all those in need and all those who are struggling.

—Kody, Providence High School, IN

Evening Prayer

Heavenly Father, the greatest act of love was shown by you on the cross. Help me to portray the love you showed us to all those I meet each day.

—Elizabeth, Notre Dame-Cathedral Latin
High School, OH

Morning Prayer

God, your love is like an evergreen: sturdy, beautiful, and always alive. I praise you.

—Delia, Saint Mary Academy, RI

Midday Prayer

I pray, Lord, for all those who find themselves doubting their abilities.

—Marissa, Epiphany Church, OK

Evening Prayer

Help me to love others the way you love me: unconditionally.

—Denise, Saint Elizabeth of Hungary
High School, TX

Morning Prayer

Please help my family to enjoy their day and end their day safely. Lord, please give my family wisdom and strength to tolerate all the problems we may face.

—Oh, Cotter High School, MN

Midday Prayer

Jesus, I pray for the friends who help keep us strong even when everything seems wrong.

—Anne, Saint John the Baptist Church , IA

Evening Prayer

Thank you, Lord Jesus, for all that you have done for me, from providing me with a good education to allowing me to live another day.

—Allison, Saint Elizabeth of Hungary
High School, TX

Morning Prayer

Lord, please show your love for me today and every day.

—Sarah, Good Shepherd Church, VA

Midday Prayer

Let us all pray for nature to guide us, rivers to heal us, and the sun to shine for us. God, help us to see and feel your love in our world.

—Antonia, DeLaSalle High School, MN

Evening Prayer

Even if I do not always love myself, you, God, and others love me. Help me to fix my brokenness.

—Natalie, Saint Francis Borgia Regional High School, MO

Morning Prayer

Lord, please fill my life with laughter.

—Kendra, Cotter High School, MN

Midday Prayer

I offer this prayer for anyone struggling with an addiction.

—Andy, Saint Charles Church, OH

Evening Prayer

Thanks be to you, God, who brings compassion, trust, and love to the earth, for this love carries on.

—Connor, Saint Ambrose Church, IN

Morning Prayer

Dear Jesus, please watch over me and keep me safe.

—Megan, Mount Saint Mary Church, OK

Midday Prayer

I pray for students in these upcoming weeks, that they may find the strength and focus to carry out the end of the school year.

—Haley, Providence High School, IN

Evening Prayer

Lord, may I strive to encourage others to reach their potential.

—Anonymous

Morning Prayer

Lord, may everyone know that they are loved today and all days.

—Katie, Prince of Peace Church, MD

Midday Prayer

I pray for all those who are unheard or unrepresented, and everyone who needs a prayer.

—Allie, Saint Barnabas Church, OH

Evening Prayer

Thank you, God, for never giving up on me.

—Hector, Waukesha West High School, WI

Morning Prayer

Dear Jesus, I am talking to you today not to ask you for anything, but to thank you for everything you have given me.

—Lauren, Holy Family Church, WI

Midday Prayer

I pray that every child will be forever loved.

—Baylee, Immaculate Conception Church, IA

Evening Prayer

Lord, may I always be there for others when they are going through tough times.

—Meghan, Saint Paul Church, MN

Morning Prayer

God, help me to remember to "ASAP": Always Say A Prayer.

—Anonymous, Saint Catherine of
Alexandria Church, MA

Midday Prayer

I pray today for those who are lost out there and can't find the hope or the love they need.

—Taylor, KS

Evening Prayer

Lord, help those who are hurt by words and actions, especially my words and actions. May they be forgiving.

—Brendyn, Saint Mary Church, MO

Morning Prayer

Give me the strength to do what is right, O God.

—Sophia, Our Lady of the Angels Church, MN

Midday Prayer

I pray for those who can no longer face the mirror, that they realize they are made in your image, God.

—Faithe, Walsh Jesuit High School, OH

Evening Prayer

I pray for the spreading of your Word, God.

—Brett, Sabetha High School, KS

Morning Prayer

God, help me to do the right thing, even if it means others won't like it.

—Josh, Sacred Heart Church, KS

Midday Prayer

I pray that all who face temptations will find your grace, Lord.

—Alex, Saint Edward Church, IN

Evening Prayer

May all those people who are drifting away from their faith find you once more, God.

—Maria, FL

Morning Prayer

Lord, help me to open my eyes to you.

—Zachary, Sacred Heart Church, KS

Midday Prayer

Lord, please protect all the people and animals in the world.

—Nicole, Saint Joseph Church, IN

Evening Prayer

Please God, keep me loved and happy.

—Katelyn, Saint John the Baptist Church, MN

Morning Prayer

Lord, help me to remember that you are with me everyday, every hour, and that I must look to you.

—Taylor, Immaculate Conception Church, NY

Midday Prayer

I pray for all those receiving the Sacrament of Confirmation.

—Benny, Saint Elizabeth of Hungary
High School, TX

Evening Prayer

For those whose lives are falling apart, Lord, help me to help them.

—Alli, Saint Patrick Church, IL

Morning Prayer

Dear Lord, please help me to be the best I can every day.

—Joanie, Incarnation Church, OH

Midday Prayer

I pray for those in need of faith and in need of motivation to be happy and to follow your Son, our Savior Jesus Christ.

—Caroline, Saint Gabriel Church, IN

Evening Prayer

Thank you, God, for giving me the opportunity to become an adult member of the Church.

—Reilly, Saint Catherine of
Alexandria Church, MA

Morning Prayer

I pray for perseverance and continued good work this day.

—Amanda, Saint Bernadette Church, KY

Midday Prayer

May we rely more on you, God, and less on technology.

—Leah, Saint Ann Church, KS

Evening Prayer

Give me the courage, Lord, to never be afraid to try something new.

—Maria, Sacred Heart Church, IN

Morning Prayer

God, help me to not worry about the past, but rather to focus on the future.

—Stephen, Saint Francis of Assisi Church, OH

Midday Prayer

For those who are searching for their vocation, I pray.

—Julie, Seton High School, OH

Evening Prayer

Lord, please show my friends and family the way to happiness.

—Eli, Saint Therese Church, PA

Morning Prayer

Jesus, help me to remember to not be afraid to do whatever your heart wants of me.

—José, Blessed Teresa Church, KY

Midday Prayer

Lord, bring all people a greater understanding of the importance of community service.

—Brad, Saint Ignatius Church, MD

Evening Prayer

You tell us that faith can move mountains. Let me truly believe this, Lord.

—Gabriela, Saint Bernard Church, IN

Morning Prayer

May my faith in you grow stronger and stronger,
O God.

—Nicole, Holy Family Church, FL

Midday Prayer

I pray for the lost and wandering, that one day
they will find your love, Lord.

—Claire, Saint Ignatius Church, MD

Evening Prayer

Jesus Christ, thank you for my friends who are
always there for me, and please bless them.

—Abigail, Saint Michael Church, OH

Morning Prayer

Lord, let me always keep my head up, stay strong, and know that I am loved.

—Kathleen, Saint Mary Church, IN

Midday Prayer

I offer this prayer for all families struggling with separation.

—Jordan, Immaculate Conception Church, OH

Evening Prayer

Thank you, Lord, for a thankful heart.

—Samantha, Saint Joseph Church, MI

Morning Prayer

Be with me, Lord, in the midst of all the pressure of school and friends.

—Sam, Saint Ignatius Church, MD

Midday Prayer

I pray for all of those who are suffering from hunger; may their hunger be satisfied.

—Christine, Saint Cecilia Church, MN

Evening Prayer

Bless, O Lord, all creatures great and small, and keep our world safe for all.

—Abbie, Saint Mary Church, MI

Morning Prayer

God, I ask that you keep me and my family safe
this day.

—Natalie, Saint Martha Church, KY

Midday Prayer

Heavenly Lord, I pray for those who haven't found
a voice to stand up for themselves or their beliefs.

—Kathryn, Saint Raphael Church, IL

Evening Prayer

I praise you, God, for being there for me through
all times.

—Elizabeth, Most Pure Heart of
Mary Church, KS

Morning Prayer

I pray to you, Father in Heaven, that the hearts of many young and old will feel loved today.

—Mary, Saint Joseph Church, MI

Midday Prayer

May all people facing natural disasters in our world today find safety and shelter.

—Kyra, Holy Family Church, MI

Evening Prayer

Teach us, Lord, to stand strong when life changes and to know that you are with us always.

—Nathan, Holy Family Church, IN

Morning Prayer

Help me, God, to be who I want to be.

—Maria, Saint Anthony of Padua Church, IN

Midday Prayer

I pray today for anyone who feels hurt.

—Allie, Saint John Neumann Church, MD

Evening Prayer

Lord, protect me and my friends and family from all evil.

—Faith, Saint Thomas More Church, KY

Morning Prayer

Help me, God, to remember that you will always be there in my darkest times, even if nobody else is.

—Anna, Most Pure Heart Church, KS

Midday Prayer

Lord, I pray for those who are bullied, that they will overcome their fears and situations.

—Daniel, Saint Francis Cathedral, NJ

Evening Prayer

Thank you, God, for the hope that you give me to complete the goals that I want in life.

—Jack, Saint Catherine of Alexandria Church, MA

Morning Prayer

May all people believe in one another and help the less fortunate.

—Hattie, Saint Aloysius Church, IA

Midday Prayer

God, be with all young people who feel ostracized from their peers.

—Kyra, Our Mother of Mercy Church, TX

Evening Prayer

God, thank you for being with me, loving me, and forgiving me.

—Allison, Saint Stephen Deacon and
Martyr Church, IL

Morning Prayer

Thank you, Lord, for bringing me to this place in my life.

—Bri, Saint Clara Church, MN

Midday Prayer

My prayer is for all soldiers and veterans who willingly give of themselves and sacrifice for others.

—Peter, Sacred Heart of Jesus Church, OH

Evening Prayer

God, help us to stand up for one another.

—Katelyn, TX

Morning Prayer

Lord, keep my family safe as they go about their day.

—Brandon, Saint Mary Church, MI

Midday Prayer

God, please keep close to your heart those who struggle with destructive addictions.

—Stephanie, Saint Francis Borgia Regional High School, MO

Evening Prayer

For all those questioning their faith, may they find their way, O God.

—Kate, Saint Benedict Church, SC

Morning Prayer

Dear God, please watch over us in our effort to serve you.

—Chloe, Saint Patrick Church, IN

Midday Prayer

Bless all the sick, that they may feel your comfort and love.

—Amy, Sacred Heart Church, OH

Evening Prayer

Lord, help me to love you with my complete heart before I love my future spouse.

—Sam, Good Shepherd Church, GA

Morning Prayer

God, give me the ability to hold true to my beliefs, and be with me in my decisions.

—Colin, Holy Spirit Church, KY

Midday Prayer

For all of our world leaders and world leaders to come, I pray.

—Sam, Sacred Heart Church, OH

Evening Prayer

Lord, take my empty heart and fill it till it overflows.

—Bernadette, Saint Dunstan Basilica, CA

Morning Prayer

Lord, I ask for the wisdom to know the difference between lust and love.

—Thomas, Saint Elizabeth Church, MA

Midday Prayer

Please keep all people from harm this day, O God.

—Shalana, DeLaSalle High School, MN

Evening Prayer

For everyone struggling to find you, Lord, I offer this prayer.

—Gabby, Owensboro Catholic High School, KY

Morning Prayer

Lord, may I affect one person's faith for the better today.

—Paige, Saint Stephen Church, KY

Midday Prayer

I pray for the people who are having a difficult time with family.

—Katie, Saint Francis Borgia Regional
High School, MO

Evening Prayer

Dear God, please give the gift of friendship to everyone.

—Lauren, Saint Peter Church, MN

Morning Prayer

Holy Spirit, help all who need your love and guidance.

—Adam, MO

Midday Prayer

For those who die from being pressured into horrible choices, I pray, O Lord.

—Robert, La Salle High School, OH

Evening Prayer

May all who believe embrace faith openly.

—Emma, Saint Mark Church, MD

Morning Prayer

Lord, may I be open to my calling and fulfill your plan for me.

—Abbey, Saint Elizabeth Ann Seton
Church, IN

Midday Prayer

Dear Lord, please help to guide those who turn to self harm.

—Katie, Saint Ludmila Church, IA

Evening Prayer

Please help us, God, to realize that you will never leave our side.

—Jillian, Saint Jude Church, PA

Morning Prayer

Lord, be with those looking to further and
strengthen their faith.

—Luis, Saint Philip Church, CT

Midday Prayer

I offer this prayer for our armed forces, that they
may be safe and know that they are in the hearts
and minds of many people.

—Natalie, Providence High School, IN

Evening Prayer

Thank you, God, for always being there for me.

—Nick, Saint Catherine of
Alexandria Church, MA

Morning Prayer

Help me today, O God, to feel the light of Christ.

—Isaac, Saints Peter and Paul Church, KS

Midday Prayer

For those who do not have the needed finances to support themselves or their families, I pray.

—Cameron, Saint Ambrose Church, IN

Evening Prayer

Give me the strength to carry on, Lord.

—Lauren, Saint Jude Church, PA

Morning Prayer

Lord, may I have the courage to follow your will and do what I know is right.

—Kristin, Saint Peter Church, MO

Midday Prayer

I offer my prayer for all those who have no one to pray for them.

—Sara, Saint Patrick Church, IA

Evening Prayer

Give me a fire of faith God, and may it burn bright and warm for all to see and feel.

—Milee, Saint Philip Church, CT

Morning Prayer

Lord, help me to be strong for those who have no strength this day.

—Austin, Sacred Heart Church, IA

Midday Prayer

For people who are suffering from a loss of a family member or friend, let them feel your peace, Lord.

—Nikki, Cotter High School, MN

Evening Prayer

I offer this prayer for all people in need of God's blessing.

—Danielle, Saint Mary Church, IA

Morning Prayer

Lord, guide me on the right path.

—Morgan, Saint Pius X Church, OH

Midday Prayer

Be with all those young people who are suffering from any sort of abuse. Give them peace.

—Jake, Saint Declan Church, Australia

Evening Prayer

God, give us the strength to reject all evil.

—Michael, Saint Francis Borgia Regional
High School, MO

Morning Prayer

I pray for all in need of your light, love, spirit, and hope in whatever challenge they're facing in life.

—DeDee, Holy Family Catholic Church, TX

Midday Prayer

God, please shine your light upon the oppressed, that they may find your strength, guidance, and love.

—Ellie, DeLaSalle High School, MN

Evening Prayer

Lord, help!

—Aline, Central Catholic High School, OH

Morning Prayer

God, please help others to respect and accept my Catholic beliefs.

—Anna, Saint Mary Church, IA

Midday Prayer

May all people have a warm place to sleep at night, O Lord.

—Justin, Providence High School, IN

Evening Prayer

Lord, help me to remember that even on my darkest days you are my bright light.

—Marcus, Saint Francis Borgia Regional High School, MO

Morning Prayer

Dear God, I'd like to ask for the motivation to do my schoolwork on time and to participate in Sunday Mass more.

—Sebastian, Cotter High School, MN

Midday Prayer

For those who are lost and can't find meaning in life, I pray.

—Katharine, Saint Francis Borgia Regional High School, MO

Evening Prayer

Lord, help all young people to never become spiritually hungry.

—Joel, Saint Teresa Church, NY

Morning Prayer

God, please let every single person find friends who will help them to grow in healthy ways.

—Austin, Pacelli High School, WI

Midday Prayer

I pray for the ones who have suffered from the bad things in life.

—Antonio, Saint Benedict High School, IL

Evening Prayer

Lord, help me to wait for the one you choose for me and to let the others pass me by.

—Carolyn, Saint Francis of Assisi Church, CO

Morning Prayer

Jesus, help me and my peers to understand what your will is for us so we can grow in your love as a stronger community.

—Jacob, Saint Francis Borgia Regional
High School, MO

Midday Prayer

I pray for the sick and lonely. Be with them, Lord.

—Breanah, Saint Elizabeth of Hungary
High School, TX

Evening Prayer

Dear God, may all teenagers who think they are not good enough for the world receive love and kindness from others.

—Lindsay, Saint Mary Church, FL

Morning Prayer

Guide me, Lord, to overcome any peer pressure I might face today.

—Rachel, Saint Louis Church, IN

Midday Prayer

I pray for those who feel any type of pain.

—Olivia, Saint Bartholmew Church, IN

Evening Prayer

Jesus, help me to learn your will for me, that I may glorify you with every part of my life.

—Nate, Saint Paul the Apostle Church, IL

Morning Prayer

God, please help me to have a great day filled with happiness and hope.

—Jessie, Holy Family Church, IN

Midday Prayer

Lord, be with all those struggling with cancer.

—Cameron, Blessed Mother Church, KY

Evening Prayer

I pray for people who are in need of direction in their lives, that they may have faith in you, God.

—Paloma, Saint Elizabeth of Hungary
High School, TX

Morning Prayer

Lord, please help and guide me on the path of my future.

—Fiona, Sacred Heart of Jesus Church, OH

Midday Prayer

I pray for those who have lost someone important to them. May they find comfort and peace in you, God.

—Sarah, Chapman High School, KS

Evening Prayer

Dear God, I thank you for all of your gifts, especially the gifts of life and happiness.

—Caitlin, Cotter High School, MN

Morning Prayer

Lord, help me to remember to pray until something happens.

—Anonymous, Saint Catherine of
Alexandria Church, MA

Midday Prayer

May the voices of unborn babies be heard. For this I pray.

—Kyle, Blessed Sacrament Church, MI

Evening Prayer

God, please watch over our grandparents as their health starts to fade, and help all families to accept this part of life.

—Collin, Saint Francis Borgia Regional
High School, MO

Morning Prayer

I offer this prayer for those who lack what they need in day-to-day life.

—Nathan, Saint Francis Borgia Regional
High School, MO

Midday Prayer

For those struggling with recovery from natural disasters, I pray. May they be provided with what they need to move forward.

—Austin, Our Lady of Mount Carmel Church, IL

Evening Prayer

Jesus, thank you for giving me a family who says, "Teasing is the way to loving."

—Sami Kay, Pacelli High School, WI

Morning Prayer

Dear God, please give me and my family the strength to bond in our love of Jesus Christ.

—Josh, Saint Francis Borgia Regional
High School, MO

Midday Prayer

I pray for all teenagers who are filled with guilt; may they realize that you, God, offer forgiveness to all.

—Claire, Saint Mary and Patrick Church, IA

Evening Prayer

I pray for anyone who is sick.

—Anna, DeLaSalle High School, MN

Morning Prayer

Please, God, give me the strength to hold onto my relationships with others.

—Colette, Cotter High School, MN

Midday Prayer

For those who cannot pray for themselves, I pray.

—Maureen, Saint Brigid of Kildare Church, OH

Evening Prayer

Loving and powerful God, you are awesome. I thank you for our families, churches, parishes, and anything else we hold in our hearts.

—David, Cotter High School, MN

Morning Prayer

I pray that Jesus will work through me this day.

—Bethany, Saint Mary Church, IA

Midday Prayer

I offer this prayer for everyone who is struggling with depression and anxiety.

—Abby, Saint Margaret Mary Church, IL

Evening Prayer

Lord, may we always stay close to our family, for they will never abandon us.

—Sarah, Good Shepherd Church, VA

Morning Prayer

Lord, may happiness one day fill every inch of the world.

—Marian, DelaSalle High School, MN

Midday Prayer

I pray for all soldiers and for the families they leave behind.

—Zach, Saint Peter Church, MO

Evening Prayer

Thank you, Jesus, for life.

—Tayshawn, Providence High School, IN

Morning Prayer

Lord, help me to always have happiness in my days, and may the sad days pass me by quickly.

—Makeba, Saint Benedict High School, IL

Midday Prayer

I offer this prayer for all people who are suffering with some form of phobia.

—Kelsie, Saint Therese Church, CO

Evening Prayer

Dear God, bless us with caring family and friends, and may we return the love and care.

—Jaclyn, Providence High School, IN

Morning Prayer

I pray that my family will have great years of life together.

—Elza, Holy Angels Church, IN

Midday Prayer

I pray that all children in the world seek refuge from violence and are able to enjoy the freedom of expression in peace and safety.

—Rob, Marist College Canberra, Australia

Evening Prayer

God, please grant your peace to those who need it most.

—Chris, Saint Francis Borgia Regional High School, MO

Morning Prayer

For the future, I pray.

—Margaret, Epiphany of Our Lord Church, OK

Midday Prayer

I pray for peace.

—Andre, Cotter High School, MN

Evening Prayer

Jesus, help all who have hardships to find hope in you.

—Megan, Immaculate Conception Church, IA

Morning Prayer

Lord, help me to see others as you see them.

—Anonymous

Midday Prayer

May the self-esteem of all children throughout the world be lifted high by your grace and loving compassion, O God.

—Michael, La Salle High School, OH

Evening Prayer

I pray for an end to abortion and for all to recognize the importance of life.

—Claire, Bishop Watterson High School, OH

Morning Prayer

Lord, let all people love one another.

—Sarah, Saint John Church, OH

Midday Prayer

I pray for all mistreated and abused animals.

—Brandon, Saint Elizabeth of Hungary
High School, TX

Evening Prayer

Lord, give sight to those who are too busy focusing on themselves that they miss all the good in others.

—Madison, Saint Francis Borgia Regional
High School, MO

Morning Prayer

Lord, please help those in need—not just me,
but all people who need something to give them
hope.

—James, Pacelli High School, WI

Midday Prayer

Lord, help us to do something to relieve all the
suffering in the world.

—Aidan, John Carroll High School, FL

Evening Prayer

God, please guide me to make the right college
decisions, and guide me to the job I am meant to
have.

—Cassie, Saint John Church, MI

Morning Prayer

Lord, please help me to keep you in my heart, even if others disccourage me from doing so.

—Amanda, Christ Our Redeemer Church, FL

Midday Prayer

I pray for those who fear to be themselves, that they find the courage to show the world who they truly are.

—Gem, Saint Joseph's Institution International, Singapore

Evening Prayer

Dear God, please give the gift of your faith to those who need you the most.

—Nikole, Saint Peter Church, MN

Morning Prayer

Today, Lord, help me to strive for progress, not perfection.

—Norah, DeLaSalle High School, MN

Midday Prayer

I pray for those who feel alone and confused about the road ahead.

—Janie, Saint Francis Borgia Regional
High School, MO

Evening Prayer

Lord, thank you for being there for me when I was feeling at my lowest.

—Hannah, DeLaSalle High School, MN

Morning Prayer

God, liberate me from stress, and bring me to peace and harmony by your side.

—Juan, Xavier High School, NY

Midday Prayer

I pray that people know they are never alone in their struggle.

—Matt, Saint Mary of Vernon Church, IL

Evening Prayer

Dear God, please help me in my time of doubt, and at all times, to see that I am exactly who you want me to be and that no matter what others think, I am beautiful in all ways.

—Elizabeth, Saint Francis Borgia Regional High School, MO

Morning Prayer

For those who feel they are not good enough, help them, Lord, to realize that they are more than enough.

—Jessie, Christ the King Church, GA

Midday Prayer

I pray for all the people around the world who can't have an education and for those who don't have a voice to fight for one.

—Olivia, Cotter High School, MN

Evening Prayer

Lord, help me to have better self-esteem and never to compare myself to others.

—Elena, PA

Morning Prayer

I pray for the strength within myself to make the right decisions, regardless of what people think.

—Ben, Saint Francis Borgia Regional
High School, MO

Midday Prayer

I pray for all the kids who don't know what they want to do with their lives.

—Brandon, Ben Davis High School, IN

Evening Prayer

Dear God, thank you for giving me the strength to get over the hurdles in life.

—Miranda, Saint Elizabeth of Hungary
High School, TX

Morning Prayer

Lord, give me guidance through the day.

—Andrew, Saint Edward Church, IN

Midday Prayer

Lord, please help all those who are trying to push through some form of psychological torment.

—Andrew, Saint Francis Borgia Regional
High School, MO

Evening Prayer

I pray for the people who cannot see the beauty they radiate, and I pray that you, God, can help them to find that beauty.

—Emily, Sacred Heart Church, Australia

Morning Prayer

Lord, help me and those I love to find our inner strength through you.

—Olivia, Saint Pius X Church, IN

Midday Prayer

Lord, we pray for the sick and their family and friends.

—John, Saint Francis Borgia Regional
High School, MO

Evening Prayer

For every girl who thinks she is not good enough, may she know that she is made in the image of God and that she is amazing.

—Geneva, Saint Michael Church, KS

Morning Prayer

Lord, may everyone who feels insignificant or bad about themselves realize how awesome and loved they are.

—Nicole, Prince of Peace Church, MD

Midday Prayer

Lord God, may all teens find caring and loving friends.

—Caitlin, Sacred Heart Church, AK

Evening Prayer

Lord, please send us strength and courage to be ourselves.

—Annmarie, Holy Spirit Church, IN

Morning Prayer

With your guiding hand, Lord Jesus, please help me to learn today what I need to know to serve you and your Kingdom tomorrow.

—Iain, La Salle High School, OH

Midday Prayer

Lord, watch over all of your creation, and guide us to make sound decisions and proper judgment.

—Daniel, John Carroll High School, FL

Evening Prayer

God, help me to be who you want me to be and not necessarily who the world expects me to be.

—Cameron, Saint Francis Borgia Regional High School, MO

Morning Prayer

Lord, help me to see my life's struggles not simply as hardships that must be endured but rather as opportunities to grow in your love.

—Andrew, Saint Francis Borgia Regional
High School, MO

Midday Prayer

Lord, please bring our soldiers home to us, safe and secure.

—Brian, Delone High School, PA

Evening Prayer

God, allow me to realize that beauty comes from within, and that with my internal beauty, I can help to make the entire world truly beautiful again.

—Rachel, Notre Dame-Cathedral Latin
High School, OH

Morning Prayer

God, help me to be courageous and humble during the day.

—Mollie, Delone High School, PA

Midday Prayer

I pray today, Lord, for all those who need a prayer.

—Charlie, DeLaSalle High School, MN

Evening Prayer

Lord, I pray for those who are suffering, for those who have strayed from you, for those who are poor, and for us, for we are sinners.

—Mary, Cotter High School, MN

Morning Prayer

Dear Lord, please give me the strength to use my talents to help those in need.

—Logan, Cotter High School, MN

Midday Prayer

I pray for all priests and seminarians, that they will lead the Church into complete devotion to you, Lord, and help to spread the power of the Eucharist to others.

—Timothy, Cotter High School, MN

Evening Prayer

Bless those who are in a constant, everyday struggle, fighting and battling for their lives every minute of every day.

—McCrae, Cotter High School, MN

Morning Prayer

I offer this prayer for anyone, young or old, who is going through depression or rough times.

—Dillon, Our Lady of Lourdes Church, KY

Midday Prayer

Dear Lord, help teens to have the courage to stand up to bullying.

—Riley, Holy Family Church, MO

Evening Prayer

God, please help those who live in a world of sorrow and pain to live in peace and harmony.

—Jorge, DeLaSalle High School, MN

Morning Prayer

Dear God, words cannot express my admiration for you, so I will live out my faith in your name.

—Anthony, DeLaSalle High School, MN

Midday Prayer

I offer this prayer today for aspiring musicians.

—Nicolet, Our Lady of Mercy Church, IL

Evening Prayer

O God, let me give hope to all who are in need.

—Will, Holy Family Church, TX

Morning Prayer

I pray for the ability to stay organized, do well, and make new friends.

—David, DeLaSalle High School, MN

Midday Prayer

For all those who don't believe they are good enough, God, please help them to see how beautiful and special they really are.

—Molly, Saint Teresa Academy, MO

Evening Prayer

For all teens who are struggling to find God in their lives, I pray.

—Marin, Immaculate Conception Church, MT

Morning Prayer

Lord, give me faith and trust in you.

—Andy, Cathedral of Helena, MT

Midday Prayer

God, help guide mothers who are considering abortion to choose life instead.

—Madeline, Saint Ann Church, IN

Evening Prayer

For all people living without the love, support, and attention of family, I pray.

—Grace, Saint Patrick Church, IN

Morning Prayer

Lord, this morning please be with all those I love who are sick.

—Audrey, Saint Michael Church, OH

Midday Prayer

I pray for my family, that they will always be linked to my love and relationship to God.

—Emily, Immaculate Conception Church, IA

Evening Prayer

My prayer is for all those who are suffering from natural disasters, that they find comfort and love.

—John, Saint Charles Borromeo, MT

Morning Prayer

God, give me hope and faith, and lead me through any hardships I face today.

—Skarleth, Saint Dominic Church, KY

Midday Prayer

Lord, please give your grace and kindness to our enemies and help us to love everyone by seeing Jesus in all people, just as you do.

—Bridget, Saint Francis Borgia Regional High School, MO

Evening Prayer

I offer my prayer for those who need patience.

—Anonymous, TX

Morning Prayer

Good morning, God. Can you please give
guidance to those who feel lost?

—Rachel, Immaculate Conception Church, IN

Midday Prayer

Lord, may we have compassion and acceptance
for one another in every community and race.

—Kayla, Holy Spirit Church, NY

Evening Prayer

Please help us to bring equality to our world.

—Alissa, Good Shepherd Church, TX

Morning Prayer

I pray, Lord, for the conversions of all those who don't know or love you.

—Rebecca, Saint Ignatius Church, MD

Midday Prayer

For the ones who do wrong, help them to see your ways, O God.

—Justin, Saint Francis Borgia Regional High School, MO

Evening Prayer

Lord, please bring rain and snow to the areas experiencing drought.

—Taylor, Saint Anthony Church, WY

Morning Prayer

God, please be with those who are confused about their future.

—Alyssa, Seton High School, OH

Midday Prayer

Lord, help us to work for peace in all of the world.

—Sang-Hyuk, Cotter High School, MN

Evening Prayer

Lord, help me to become a better person and to help others.

—Anonymous

Morning Prayer

Dear Lord, give me the strength to stand up for others and do what's right.

—Ali, Sacred Heart Church, MN

Midday Prayer

Lord, help us to bring down the barrirers of race, sex, nationality, and religion that divide our world.

—Sam, Marist College Canberra, Australia

Evening Prayer

Tonight I offer my prayer for all those in need of serious medical attention.

—Cody, Holy Spirit Church, KY

Morning Prayer

God, please help teens to be okay with being
themselves even under peer pressure.

—Anonymous

Midday Prayer

I pray, O God, for all those people who are lost
and need you.

—Bridgett, Saint James Church, KY

Evening Prayer

When I think that nobody cares, remind me, Lord,
to take a long, hard look at a crucifix.

—Logan, Saint John the Baptist Church, OH

Morning Prayer

I pray for all those who don't have a warm place to stay.

—Anonymous, Saint Catherine of Alexandria Church, MA

Midday Prayer

Lord, renew my hope in humanity.

—Lorenzo, Saint John Vianney Church, MI

Evening Prayer

Lord, I am thankful for my family, who is there for me every day.

—Michaela, Cotter High School, MN

Morning Prayer

God, thank you for the gift of my grandparents.
Watch over them always.

—Andrew, Saint Elizabeth of Hungary
High School, TX

Midday Prayer

Lord, please be with those who struggle with low
self-confidence and depression.

—Kaylee, Saint Elizabeth Ann Seton
Church, IL

Evening Prayer

I pray for my future spouse, if I have one.

—Melanie, Holy Childhood of Jesus Church, IL

Morning Prayer

God, help me to never forget that someone loves me and that happiness is never too far away.

—Haley, Holy Spirit Church, IN

Midday Prayer

I pray for the will of humankind, that it will strive for peace.

—Patrick, Saint Barnabas Church, IN

Evening Prayer

I offer this prayer for those who have a hard time living with their parents.

—Logan, Saint Francis Borgia Regional High School, MO

Morning Prayer

Good morning, God. Today help me to be myself and to remember that our world is made up of unique individuals just like me.

—Connor, Cotter High School, MN

Midday Prayer

Dear God, I pray for all of the sick people in the world.

—Christopher, LA

Evening Prayer

Thank you, God, for my caring church community.

—Alissa, Good Shepherd Church, TX

Morning Prayer

Lord, I pray for all those who live with physical and emotional disabilities.

—Anonymous

Midday Prayer

Bless all all those battling cancer, O God.

—Rachel, Mount Saint Mary Church, OK

Evening Prayer

Thank you, Lord, for moments of failure that teach us important lessons.

—Victoria, Cotter High School, MN

Morning Prayer

Dear God, please help me to understand your plan for my life.

—Carissa, Saint Francis Borgia Regional High School, MO

Midday Prayer

Lord, help us to work to end homelessness in our communities.

—Mary, Incarnation Church, IL

Evening Prayer

My prayer is for those who have trouble believing in themselves.

—Jordan, Guardian Angels Central High School, NE

Morning Prayer

Dear God, thank you for making me amazing and giving me a special meaning in this world.

—Sara, Blessed Trinity Church, MI

Midday Prayer

My prayer is for all those who are suffering in body, mind, or spirit.

—Katie, Saint Elizabeth of Hungary
High School, TX

Evening Prayer

Grant me a restful sleep tonight, O God.

—Laura, Saint Anthony Church, TX

Morning Prayer

Lord, give me the strength to do the best that I can for others.

—Sergio, DeLaSalle High School, MN

Midday Prayer

I offer my prayer for all of those who are struggling to make ends meet.

—Abbey, Saint Francis Borgia Regional
High School, MO

Evening Prayer

God, thank you for the opportunity to thank you.

—Kylie, Saint James Church, NY

Morning Prayer

God, may I truly know that Jesus loves me for who I am, not what I look like.

—Sara, Blessed Trinity Church, MI

Midday Prayer

Dear Lord, please help those who feel alone and by themselves.

—T. J., Notre Dame-Cathedral Latin High School, OH

Evening Prayer

God, I pray that the strength of family is stronger than any hardships a family may face.

—Cartes, Blessed Sacrament Church, MI

Morning Prayer

Lord, I am faced with obstacles, but you know
I can handle them, so guide me and give me
strength to carry on.

—Abigail, Saint Francis Borgia Regional
High School, MO

Midday Prayer

I pray for those who will be on the streets all
winter, that they will find shelter to keep themselves
warm.

—Jacob, Mary of the Visitation Church, MN

Evening Prayer

No matter how much suffering we endure, may
you, Lord, remind us that we are worthy of your
love.

—Miguel, Saint James Church, MO

Morning Prayer

Lord, bless our world today, that it may become a more stable and safe place to live.

—Kayla, Our Mother of Mercy Church, TX

Midday Prayer

For all who feel lost, may they feel your love, God.

—Taylor, Nativity of Our Lord Church, WI

Evening Prayer

Lord, give me the strength to help others and to make a difference.

—Brianna, John Carroll High School, FL

Morning Prayer

O God, may I be happy, helpful, and humble.

—Ceci, Saint Teresa Academy, MO

Midday Prayer

Lord, please help us to end to abortion.

—Isaac, Saint John Church, KS

Evening Prayer

Thank you, Lord, for all of the veterans whose service lets us live such good lives today.

—Isaac, IA

Morning Prayer

Dear God, help me to live for other people's happiness and not just my own so that I can follow in the footsteps of Christ.

—Carlie, Providence High School, IN

Midday Prayer

God, help the ones who think they are alone to realize that it's more than just them against the world.

—Emily, Saint Francis Borgia Regional High School, MO

Evening Prayer

Lord, thank you for the gift of creation. May we never abuse it or take it for granted.

—Kylie, Saint James Church, NY

Morning Prayer

For all innocent people who suffer, I pray, Lord.

—Vanessa, Providence High School, IN

Midday Prayer

I want to pray for all those who don't have what they need, that they are able to receive whatever they need most.

—Rose, DeLaSalle High School, MN

Evening Prayer

Lord, let me simply say thank you.

—Laura, Saint Anthony Church, TX

Morning Prayer

I offer my prayer this morning for all children who are sick or hospitalized.

—Caroline, Sacred Heart of Jesus
High School, OH

Midday Prayer

For all those who face learning difficulties and challenges, I pray.

—Susie, Saint Cecilia Church, FL

Evening Prayer

Dear God, please help all those who are suffering to make it through the day, and help them to realize the good things in life.

—Brooke, Saint Francis Borgia Regional
High School, MO

Morning Prayer

I offer my prayer this morning for my friends.

—Tammy, Providence High School, IN

Midday Prayer

I pray for families affected by gun violence.

—Kylie, Saint James Church, NY

Evening Prayer

Please, God, help me to have the strength to get through applying to college.

—Teresa, Saint Francis Borgia Regional
High School, MO

Morning Prayer

For all souls in need, I pray.

—Paige, Saint Ludmila Church, IA

Midday Prayer

I pray for those who struggle with being honest.

—Breanna, Saint James Church, KY

Evening Prayer

Lord, please be with all siblings and family members serving in the armed forces.

—Laura, Cotter High School, MN

Morning Prayer

God, help me to be respectful toward everyone I meet today, and always.

—Josh, Saint Robert Bellarmine Church, MO

Midday Prayer

I pray for all who feel lost.

—Rachel, Newton High School, IA

Evening Prayer

Thank you, Lord, for giving me life.

—Becca, Saint Joseph Church, MD

Morning Prayer

Today, Lord, I pray for my parents.

—Fengbo, Cotter High School, MN

Midday Prayer

God, please give comfort to all people recovering from surgery.

—Renae, Cotter High School, MN

Evening Prayer

God, may everyone seek peace in their lives.

—Brandon, Our Lady of the Pines Church, CO

Morning Prayer

Lord, please keep my family safe, sound, and happy.

—Grace, Wilmington High School, MD

Midday Prayer

I pray that youth everywhere have the courage to live out their faith.

—Mai, Saint Francis of Assissi Church, NJ

Evening Prayer

O God, please be with all parents who are suffering physical pain.

—Jared, Our Lady of Fátima Church, AR

Morning Prayer

Lord, help me to remember that my actions speak louder than my words.

—Cophie, Holy Cross Church, NE

Midday Prayer

I pray for children who have lost a parent.

—Dylan, Saint Ignatius Church, TX

Evening Prayer

You are a good and gracious God. I praise you, Lord.

—Erin, Good Shepherd Church, TX

Morning Prayer

Lord, when I am hurt by someone I care about, help me to offer true forgiveness.

—Anonymous

Midday Prayer

I pray for the protection of all soldiers who are fighting in the war.

—Sydney, Saint Elizabeth of Hungary
High School, TX

Evening Prayer

O God, may I always be willing to love and to be loved.

—Kathryn, Saint Mary Church, TN

Morning Prayer

Protect and bless me today, O God.

—Sarah, Saint Anthony Church, TX

Midday Prayer

Lord, please help to ease the suffering of the terminally ill and their loved ones.

—Bethany, Saint Francis Borgia Regional
High School, MO

Evening Prayer

I offer you thanks, Lord, for the gift of the saints, who model holy living for us.

—Dylan, Prince of Peace Church, TX

Morning Prayer

Dear Lord, may I remember that every person I meet is fighting their own battles and that I must treat them with compassion and understanding.

—Madeline, Providence High School, IN

Midday Prayer

My prayer is for all those who are homeless.

—Judy, Saint John Church, IA

Evening Prayer

Lord, please help all those who are struggling to get up each day.

—Jack, Saint Francis Borgia Regional High School, MO

Morning Prayer

Today, Lord, I will say yes to you.

—Anonymous

Midday Prayer

I pray for effective leadership, driven by conviction.

—Michael, DeLaSalle High School, MN

Evening Prayer

Lord, please give me a forgiving spirit.

—Megan, Saint Cecilia Church, FL

Morning Prayer

Lord, send your comfort to all those struggling with eating disorders.

—Jacob, Saint Ignatius Church, TX

Midday Prayer

I pray for all the people out there scared of commitment, that they will find the strength to do what God has planned for them.

—Taylor, Providence High School, IN

Evening Prayer

Lord, may I give you all of the burdens I carry this night.

—Rosanna, Saint Ignatius Church, AL

Morning Prayer

I am your servant, Lord. Use me as you see best.

—Ronnie, All Saints Church, FL

Midday Prayer

God, please help me in hard times at school.

—Israel, Saint Elizabeth of Hungary
High School, TX

Evening Prayer

Lord, only by your touch are the evil and sick
returned from the dark.

—Iggy, DeLaSalle High School, MN

Morning Prayer

I offer my prayer for all those who are faced with incurable disease.

—Susan, Our Lady of Lourdes Church, AL

Midday Prayer

Thank you, God, for gifting us with the great education system we have.

—McKenna, Upper Arlington High School, OH

Evening Prayer

Lord, please be with the brokenhearted.

—Erin, Good Shepherd Church, TX

Morning Prayer

O God, make me a person who never shuns others.

—Katie, Saint Anthony Church, OK

Midday Prayer

Lord, please help those who are suffering from domestic violence.

—Michail, Saint Francis Borgia Regional
High School, MO

Evening Prayer

Lord, take away any anger I feel.

—Mark, Saint Francis Church, AL

Morning Prayer

God, may I be open to the blessings this day will offer.

—Lisa, Saint James Church, GA

Midday Prayer

I pray for all parents who are unemployed.

—Alissa, Good Shepherd Church, NY

Evening Prayer

For the wrongly accused, I pray.

—Carlee, Saint Bartholomew Church, TX

Morning Prayer

Lord, help me to be open to change in my life.

—Katie, Our Lady of Lourdes Church, AL

Midday Prayer

I pray for the kids who are bullied every day but continue to go to school because they are strong.

—Cianna, Saint Joseph High School, PA

Evening Prayer

Give me energy, Lord, when I am feeling low and defeated.

—Emily, Saint Bartholomew Church, FL

Morning Prayer

Guide each of my steps today, Lord.

—John, Saint James Church, CA

Midday Prayer

I pray for the violence going on in schools around the world, that students can have a safe place of education and can experience love and safety from the students and faculty.

—Sam, Saint Francis Borgia Regional
High School, MO

Evening Prayer

Grant relief and comfort to all those in pain, I pray, O God.

—John, Saint Mary Church, OK

Morning Prayer

Lord, please heal all hurting and wounded hearts this day.

—Megan, Saint Elizabeth Church, CA

Midday Prayer

God, give us the courage to stand up for justice.

—Jack, Cotter High School, MN

Evening Prayer

Grant us peace, Lord.

—Anthony, Saint Michael Church, MN

Morning Prayer

When all else fails, help me, Lord, to turn to you.

—Laurie, Saint Anthony Church, NY

Midday Prayer

I pray for all those who are too afraid to stand up for themselves, that they may find strength in you, God.

—Cole, Immaculate Conception Church, MO

Evening Prayer

For those who have died today, Lord, I pray.

—Anonymous

Morning Prayer

O God, may I bring your love to someone new today.

—Mark, Sacred Heart Church, AL

Midday Prayer

Lord, I pray for all young adults to find acceptance and peace with who they are.

—Anna, Sacred Heart Church, VA

Evening Prayer

Help me to remember that nothing can separate me from your love, Lord.

—Kate, Saint Peter Church, IL

Morning Prayer

Good morning, God. Help me to make this a day you and I can be proud of.

—Carlee, Holy Spirit Church, MD

Midday Prayer

Dear Lord, please help everyone who is struggling with drug and alcohol abuse to seek out the help they need.

—Brayden, Sacred Heart Church, AK

Evening Prayer

Send your Spirit, O Lord, to all those in need this night.

—Jacob, Saint Margaret Church, NY

Morning Prayer

Make me more faithful, O God.

—Cesar, Holy Spirit Church, KY

Midday Prayer

I pray for the people who feel like they have no voice, that they have the strength to speak out.

—Katie, DeLaSalle High School, MN

Evening Prayer

For all those affected by any natural disaster, I offer this prayer.

—Quinn, Saint Pius X Church, OH

Morning Prayer

Grant me wisdom, patience, humility, and love, O Lord.

—Aidan, Saint Edward Church, AL

Midday Prayer

I pray for all kids who are experienceing the loss of a family member or friend.

—Tray, Saint Elizabeth of Hungary High School, TX

Evening Prayer

Dear God, please help our future spouses to make the right decisions.

—Emily, Saint Francis Borgia Regional High School, MO

Morning Prayer

Dear God, please allow me to find happiness in everything and anything I do.

—Nicole, Our Lady of Victory Church, FL

Midday Prayer

I pray for anyone going through a rough time right now.

—Amber, Cotter High School, MN

Evening Prayer

I offer this prayer for my family's safety and happiness.

—Hallie, Our Lady of Providence
High School, IN

Morning Prayer

Jesus, bring me courage.

—Sean, Saint Barnabas Church, IL

Midday Prayer

I pray for those who suffer from physical and emotional pain.

—Maddison, Saint Joseph Church, MN

Evening Prayer

God, help us to remember that friendship is a gift we should not take for granted.

—Sean, Saint Jude Church, AR

Morning Prayer

For families facing hard times, I pray.

—Bailey, Scecina Memorial High School, IN

Midday Prayer

Lord, please be with all those who have been hurt by someone close to them.

—Emily, Saint Francis Borgia Regional
High School, MO

Evening Prayer

I pray for those who suffer and that you, God, will help me to take on the suffering of others.

—Alex, DeLaSalle High School, MN

Morning Prayer

God, give me the strength and guidance to get me through these tough times.

—Patrick, Providence High School, IN

Midday Prayer

My prayer is for all the victims of violence around the world, for all the defenseless, and for those whose voices against violence are not heard.

—Jesica, DeLaSalle High School, MN

Evening Prayer

God, let anyone who may be suffering, for whatever reason, be free. Send your angels to guide them.

—Sean, Our Lady of Mount Carmel Church, NJ

Morning Prayer

Dear Lord, Please assist me in overcoming the setbacks, hardships, and loneliness that can happen in life.

—Mat, Delone High School, PA

Midday Prayer

Lord, help our churches to be a place of acceptance and love for all who enter them.

—Anonymous, TX

Evening Prayer

I offer this prayer for the weak at heart, that they may find the strength to find the glory in each day and learn to love themselves and find love in the world.

—Sommer, Providence High School, IN

Morning Prayer

Dear God, please help me to understand your plan for my life.

—Carissa, Saint Francis Borgia Regional
High School, MO

Midday Prayer

For all child soldiers, I offer this prayer, Lord.

—Daniel, Australia

Evening Prayer

I pray for all souls in Purgatory.

—Isaias, Saint Elizabeth of Hungary
High School, TX

Morning Prayer

God, please help those who may be having a
bad day today.

—Chelsea, Saint Francis Borgia Regional
High School, MO

Midday Prayer

May all Christians in Muslim countries find safety
and avoid persecution.

—Gabriella, Saints Peter and Paul Church, KS

Evening Prayer

Lord, open my eyes to the suffering of others.

—Paige, Providence High School, IN

Morning Prayer

God, grant me the strength and faith in you to overcome my battles and to have irrevocable faith in you always.

—Sarah, Providence High School, IN

Midday Prayer

I pray for vocations to the priesthood and religious life.

—Mason, Blessed Mother Church, KY

Evening Prayer

Give solace to all who suffer, O God.

—Kay, IN

Morning Prayer

Life is hard, but you, God, are unbreakable. Thank you.

—Joseph, Holy Spirit Church, IN

Midday Prayer

Dear Lord, I pray for everyone who does not have the opportunity to experience an education that they deserve.

—Sarah, Saint Benedict High School, IL

Evening Prayer

May the Holy Spirit guide the poor and homeless to better situations in life.

—Katie, Sacred Heart of Jesus School, OH

Morning Prayer

God, help me to know that I am always enough for you.

—Amy, Saint Gabriel Church, KY

Midday Prayer

I offer this prayer for all the kids in high school that are mistreated.

—Maddie, Providence High School, IN

Evening Prayer

Dear Lord, help me to embrace others and to show your love, even in my own grief.

—Monica, Christ the King Church, AR

Morning Prayer

God, help me with my struggles today, that I may remember you will be with me always.

—Stevie, Saint Philip Neri Church, OK

Midday Prayer

Lord, be with those who are victims of violence, especially children.

—Laura, Saint Anthony Church, TX

Evening Prayer

Bless, O God, all those who have struggles in their hearts.

—Anonymous

Morning Prayer

I pray that I can know and follow your will, Lord.

—Kate, Saint Joseph Church, MN

Midday Prayer

For all those blinded by fear, that they remember that hope can help guide them through any darkness, I pray.

—Carly, Saint Joseph Church, IL

Evening Prayer

May all violence cease, O God.

—Joshua, Holy Spirit Church, NY

Morning Prayer

Lord, work through me to help stop the violence in the world.

—Kaylee, Pacelli High School, WI

Midday Prayer

Help us to care for and love the earth and all of creation you have blessed us with, O God.

—Adam, Saint Mary Church, NE

Evening Prayer

I pray for all members of the military who are risking their lives every day.

—Leopold, HI

Morning Prayer

O Lord, please lead me to the path that you have paved for me.

—Grace, Saint Joseph Church, KY

Midday Prayer

Lord, grant direction to those who have turned their backs on you.

—Tristan, Saint Patrick Church, TN

Evening Prayer

Lord, please help me to remember that the plans you have for me are far better than anything I could ever imagine.

—Meg, Saint Paul the Apostle Church, IL

Morning Prayer

Lord Jesus, let me know your great love for me, even when it is hard to see.

—Emily, Saint John the Evangelist Church, KY

Midday Prayer

Dear God, I pray for those who are out in the street, especially those with mental illnesses.

—Kristina, Saint Pius X Church, IN

Evening Prayer

God, help me to go where I am meant to go.

—Madeline, Saint Thomas More Church, IA

Morning Prayer

Lord, give me the strength to reach my true calling through you.

—Michelle, Cotter High School, MN

Midday Prayer

We offer this prayer for all who are victims of terrorism in the world.

—Donovan and Zach, Saint Jude Church, AR

Evening Prayer

May you, Lord, watch over my family and give them strength for life.

—Kelsie, Holy Family Church, IA

Morning Prayer

Love, faith, and unity are all around us. Help me to embrace them, God.

—Jake, DeLaSalle High School, MN

Midday Prayer

I pray for all children diagnosed with cancer.

—Elizabeth, Immaculate Conception Church, MT

Evening Prayer

Lord, help me to slow down and listen to your voice, and show me where I need to go.

—Nate, Thomas More Prep High School, KS

Morning Prayer

Lord, help me to love Jesus and to serve him faithfully.

—Tommy, Christ the King Church, IN

Midday Prayer

I pray for all people who have experienced a natural disaster.

—Kenna, Saint Joseph Church, IA

Evening Prayer

Thank you, God, for blessing me with great friends and family.

—Katie, Holy Spirit Church, IN

Morning Prayer

Help me to understand your calling for my life, O Lord.

—Josh, Holy Redeemer Church, MI

Midday Prayer

For all those who have fallen away from our faith, I pray.

—Malgorsto, Saint Margaret Church, IL

Evening Prayer

I seek you, Lord, even when I cannot hear you. May I feel your presence.

—Taylor, Holy Redeemer Church, MI

Morning Prayer

God, please help me to love and to help the ones who need it.

—Tom, IL

Midday Prayer

Jesus, I pray for all teens trying to find themselves. May they succeed and discover the good things in life and the love of God.

—Mia, Saint Clare Church, OH

Evening Prayer

May I always be a thankful, kind, and loving Christian.

—Jackson, Marist College Canberra, Australia

Morning Prayer

Dear Lord, let me keep in my heart all those who are sick or injured. And thank you, God, for my health.

—Robbie, Our Lady of Providence Church, IL

Midday Prayer

I pray for the people who don't know you, Lord.

—Nicole, Saint Aloysius Church, KY

Evening Prayer

For those who have been called into the military, I offer this prayer.

—Seth, Our Lady of the Lake Church, SC

Morning Prayer

God, continue to guide me through my Christian faith.

—Sophia, Rosary Chapel, KY

Midday Prayer

I pray for those who are struggling in school.

—Parker, Saint Francis Borgia Regional
High School, MO

Evening Prayer

Thank you, Lord, for all the people in the world, each and every one of them.

—Clare, Saint Elizabeth Ann Seton
Church, MD

Morning Prayer

Lord, help me to give it my all, for it is all I have to give to you.

—Grace, Saint John Church, OH

Midday Prayer

I pray for all of the children who are bullied in school, that they may the find peace, hope, and love that is shared by their families.

—Faustina, Saint Elizabeth of Hungary
High School, TX

Evening Prayer

Thank you, God, for everything.

—Mackenzie, Saint James Church, IA

Morning Prayer

Dear Lord, please let everyone know that you have a plan for each of us, and that we must never lose hope.

—Hannah, Saint Mary Church, KS

Midday Prayer

I pray for married couples.

—Hope, Saint Vincent College, PA

Evening Prayer

Grant me, God, the concentration and ability to keep my life balanced.

—Stacy, Saint James Church, IA

Morning Prayer

Help me, Lord, to love you every day.

—Joe, Saint Michael Church, IL

Midday Prayer

Lord, help the people going through hard times to try to find you, and give them some comfort.

—Brendan, Saint Francis Borgia Regional
High School, MO

Evening Prayer

Dear Father, I offer this prayer for all children and women being abused and left for lost.

—Tiana, Our Mother of Mercy Church, TX

Morning Prayer

Although it may seem impossible, and that life keeps throwing obstacles, Lord, please give me the strength to embrace each day.

—Joe, Saint Nick Church, KS

Midday Prayer

I pray for the unhappy, that they may find gladness.

—Hannah, Mother of Sorrows Church, PA

Evening Prayer

No matter what happens, God, I know you will always be there to help me pick up the pieces. Thank you.

—Danielle, Saint Pius X Church, IN

Morning Prayer

Jesus, give me strength.

—Eli, Saint Pius X Church, KS

Midday Prayer

I pray for those trapped behind clear walls, watching happiness walk away. May they find the strength to escape their cage and reach happiness.

—Zach, Saint Francis Borgia Regional
High School, MO

Evening Prayer

God, may all of the earth seek peace.

—Brandon, Our Lady of the Pines Church, CO

Morning Prayer

When I doubt, Lord, help me to believe more fully in your love.

—Jake, IN

Midday Prayer

For all children without a family, I pray.

—Sam, Archangels Church, IA

Evening Prayer

I offer my prayer for those who don't know their place in the world.

—Nick, Our Lady Queen of
Peace Church, OH

Morning Prayer

Lord, may I use my gifts and talents to share your love today.

—Allyson, Our Lady of the Pines Church, CO

Midday Prayer

I pray for anyone who has lost a loved one, that they find comfort and peace in you, God.

—Mikala, Cotter High School, MN

Evening Prayer

Please help me to see the light at the end of the dark tunnel. I want to see you, Lord.

—Isabella, Saint Charles Borromeo Church, OH

Morning Prayer

My prayer is for everyone who has an illness.

—Laura, Saint Charles Borromeo Church, OH

Midday Prayer

May the less fortunate receive the support and help they need.

—Katie, Saint Elizabeth of Hungary
High School, TX

Evening Prayer

Lord, help me to lead my faithless friends to you.

—Anna, Saint Michael Church, MI

Morning Prayer

Lord, may I strive to be my own person and remain strong in my faith.

—Brian, Incarnation Church, OH

Midday Prayer

May all those facing rough times feel your presence, O God, and may they trust in you.

—Abby, Saint Patrick Church, TN

Evening Prayer

Lord, give me self-respect.

—Emily, Saint Joseph Church, IA

Morning Prayer

Dear God, help me to become closer to you.

—Emily, Our Lady Church, MO

Midday Prayer

For all people affected by tornadoes, hurricanes, earthquakes, tsunamis, and other natural disasters, I pray.

—Jeanne, Saint Mary of Vernon Church, IL

Evening Prayer

Thank you, Lord, for this wonderful day. May tomorrow be as blessed.

—Theresa, Our Lady of Fátima Church, AR

Morning Prayer

Give me the courage, Lord, to go and be an instrument of your peace.

—Delaney, Saint Charles Borromeo Church, IN

Midday Prayer

I pray for children of divorced families, that they know that they are loved by you, God.

—Jakob, PA

Evening Prayer

I know, Lord, that sometimes the light fades dim, but if I call, you will light the way.

—Grace, Divine Savior Church, WI

Morning Prayer

Thank you, Lord. This is my prayer.

—Lizzie, Trinity Church, IA

Midday Prayer

I pray that teens realize what love truly is and that they share their love with everyone, even enemies.

—Abby, Providence High School, IN

Evening Prayer

For the ones who get made fun of, I pray, Lord.

—Carly, Divine Savior Church, WI

Morning Prayer

Lord, please grant my entire family strength.

—Ron, Saint Alphonsus Ligouri Church, IN

Midday Prayer

God, please comfort all children who have parents with severe medical conditions.

—Samuel, Saint Francis Borgia Regional
High School, MO

Evening Prayer

Give me the grace to live a life full of you, Lord.

—Abigail, Saint Charles Borromeo Church, IN

Morning Prayer

God, help me to overcome the fears I have today
and always.

—Griffin, Saint Charles Borromeo Church, IN

Midday Prayer

For all those without a home, family, or friends, I
pray.

—Holly, Saint Clare Church, OH

Evening Prayer

Lord, please give consolation to anyone who feels
like they aren't enough.

—Noel, Sacred Heart Church, IA

Morning Prayer

Help me to grow and to seek you, Lord, even in the darkest of times.

—Brandon, Good Shepherd Church, TX

Midday Prayer

Lord, give me strength and perserverance to get through this school year.

—Natalie, Saint Francis Borgia Regional High School, MO

Evening Prayer

May I trust in your power and grace, O God.

—Ann, Saint Anthony Church, TX

Morning Prayer

I pray that all youth can find Christ's love through fellowship.

—Kathleen, Holy Family Church, FL

Midday Prayer

For all the people who feel alone and unloved, help them, Lord, to know the love of your Son.

—Kristina, Saint Clarence Church, OH

Evening Prayer

Lord, be with all those who suffer the emptiness of losing a loved one.

—Sarah, Mercy High School, MI

Morning Prayer

I pray to you, God, for a great and wonderful day.

—Collin, Saint Francis Borgia Regional
High School, MO

Midday Prayer

Thank you, Lord, for all those who have shown me the love of your Son, Jesus.

—Frank, Christ the Redeemer Church, TX

Evening Prayer

Lord, I give you thanks for friends who stand by one another even after they make poor choices.

—Meaghan, Saint Elizabeth Ann Seton
Church, IN

Morning Prayer

Lord, show me your way.

—Cat, Mount De Sales Academy, MD

Midday Prayer

For children who are not treated with respect, I pray, O God.

—Nicole, Incarnation Church, IL

Evening Prayer

Bless all those kids out there who are afraid to show they love you, Lord.

—Stephanie, Saint Elizabeth Ann Seton Church, IN

Morning Prayer

Loving God, help us to open the doors to our hearts when you come knocking.

—Karina, Saint Mary High School, KY

Midday Prayer

I pray for those who are having trouble finding their true selves and their purpose in life.

—Connie, John Carroll High School, FL

Evening Prayer

For doctors, nurses, emergency workers, and all who bring healing to others, I offer my thanks to you, Lord.

—Amy, Saint Maximilian Church, TX

Morning Prayer

Lord, let there be peace in all war-torn countries.

—Emily, Queen of Angels Church, IL

Midday Prayer

For all those who struggle to have the basic necessities in life, I pray.

—Oscar, Saint Joseph Church, WI

Evening Prayer

Dear God, give the gift of happiness to everyone who is in need of it.

—Camille, Saint Peter Church, MN

Morning Prayer

Lord, show me your plan for me, and allow me to embrace it.

—Mary, Mount De Sales Academy, MD

Midday Prayer

For all those in the last days of their lives, I offer this prayer.

—Alissa, Good Shepherd Church, TX

Evening Prayer

Dear God, help us to make bad times better.

—Kaylie, Saint Peter Church, MN

Morning Prayer

Lord, help me to choose you.

—Daniel, Saint Elizabeth Ann Seton
Church, MO

Midday Prayer

I pray for those who face mental illness, that they have the courage to get help.

—Becca, Saint John Church, MD

Evening Prayer

God, give all young people complete confidence in themselves.

—Anna, Saint Michael Church, MI

Morning Prayer

I pray that all kids will come to know Jesus one day.

—Kelsey, Owensboro Catholic High School, KY

Midday Prayer

Dear God, be with those without homes and those who are sick.

—Jamal, DeLaSalle High School, MN

Evening Prayer

Thank you, God, for the opportunity for forgiveness.

—Noah, Cotter High School, MN

Morning Prayer

May the love of God always be with me.

—Samantha, Providence High School, IN

Midday Prayer

For all the people who are in need of God's wisdom, I pray.

—Nayelli, Our Lady of Victory Church, OR

Evening Prayer

Help me, Lord, to treat everyone as the beloved.

—Lauren, Sacred Heart Church, IA

Morning Prayer

Lord, I am thankful that you are with me in all circumstances.

—Sam, Cotter High School, MN

Midday Prayer

I offer my prayer for those lacking basic necessities in life.

—Fred, Saint Mary Church, MI

Evening Prayer

Mary, pray for us. Holy Spirit, guide us. Jesus, I trust in you.

—Olivia, Mercy High School, MI

Morning Prayer

Lord, give me courage and faith to make it through this day. Help me to face my adversities and reach for the stars.

—Rachel, John Carroll High School, FL

Midday Prayer

For everyone who is suffering from sickness, I pray.

—Madison, Saint Joseph Church, MI

Evening Prayer

Though it may be cold through the night, your love keeps me warm always. I praise you, God.

—Alex, Cotter High School, MN

Morning Prayer

Dear Lord, thank you for all the blessings you have given me in my life.

—Patricia, Our Lady of Perpetual Help
Church, IN

Midday Prayer

May those who are faced with peer pressure stand strong.

—Anonymous, Saint Michael Church, MI

Evening Prayer

God, please help to guide anyone who is trying to find themselves.

—Natalie, Pacelli High School, WI

Morning Prayer

Lord, please help me to do the best that I can today.

—John, Saint Francis Borgia Regional
High School, MO

Midday Prayer

I pray for all athletes as they train, that they may use the gifts God has given them.

—Alex, Holy Spirit Church, KY

Evening Prayer

Dear God, take out any splinter that is penetrated deep in my heart that prevents me from receiving your grace or from loving others.

—Elizabeth, Saint Benedict High School, IL

Morning Prayer

I pray, Lord, that I will do the best in school for all
my classes.

—Tyrin, Saint Elizabeth Church, TX

Midday Prayer

Dear God, I give thanks for teachers who give up
their time to teach us something new.

—Mary, Cotter High School, MN

Evening Prayer

For those who struggle in hard times to have
everyday necessities, I offer this prayer.

—Cynthia, Roscommon High School, MI

Morning Prayer

Dear God, thank you for all the blessings you have given me that I frequently overlook.

—Corinne, Saint Francis Borgia Regional
High School, MO

Midday Prayer

Lord, please be with all those who are battling a mental inhibition.

—Cody, Holy Spirit Church, KY

Evening Prayer

Take from me the worries and concerns I carry, Lord, and let me rest in you.

—Anonymous, Pacelli High School, WI

Morning Prayer

Lord, help me to judge things by what they are,
not by what I perceive them to be.

—Richard, Saint Benedict High School, IL

Midday Prayer

For those who are suffering from addiction, may
they find light, O God.

—Sid, DeLaSalle High School, MN

Evening Prayer

Thank you, Lord, for this day. Please help me to
follow my dreams in life.

—Blake, Saint Francis Borgia Regional
High School, MO

Morning Prayer

I pray that all people can learn to place their pain and suffering in your hands, O God.

—Maria, Saint Thomas More Church, KY

Midday Prayer

I pray for every girl out there who is struggling with self-esteem.

—Morgan, Our Lady of the Pines Church, CO

Evening Prayer

To run and not be weary and walk and not be faint, I ask for your strength, Lord.

—Rachel, Saint Mary High School, OR

Morning Prayer

Dear Jesus, help me to better myself so that I can have the willpower to help others in need, and to not take out my anger on others when I have had a bad day.

—Alex, Saint Francis Borgia Regional
High School, MO

Midday Prayer

I pray for those who believe no one cares. We all do, every day.

—Kirby, Saint William of York Church, MD

Evening Prayer

When temptation comes my way, help me to avoid it, Lord. For strength, I pray.

—Gabriel, Saint Mary's Springs Academy, WI

Morning Prayer

Father, grant me the wings I need to soar far above the world and its ways so that I may see and follow your plan for me.

—Amanda, Saint Helen Church, OH

Midday Prayer

Please help those who cannot find shelter in these conditions, and allow us to find the love to help those in need.

—Eli, DeLaSalle High School, MN

Evening Prayer

Lord, I pray for happiness.

—B., Saint Ben Church, IL

Morning Prayer

Dear God, sometimes we are blinded by all of the difficulties we have to face. Please help us to see the beauty in all things.

—Abigail, MN

Midday Prayer

My prayer is for those who deserve the sun but only get the pouring rain.

—Matt, Providence High School, IN

Evening Prayer

God, help us all to find peace in our lives.

—Emily, Sacred Heart of Jesus Church, OH

Morning Prayer

Jesus, help me to be more like you in making the right choices when I am faced with the temptations that life brings.

—Kennedy, Bishop Grimes High School, NY

Midday Prayer

We pray for everyone who is struggling with world hunger, disasters, violence, and illness.

—Kylie and Carli, Saint Ann Church, MN

Evening Prayer

Dear God, please understand that I am confused and frustrated. Everything seems to fall apart at once. I'm trying my best. I promise.

—Grace, Saint Francis Borgia Regional High School, MO

Morning Prayer

God, thank you for rain, snow, sleet, and hail;
bales of hay and snowy trails; those cows, sheep,
and pigs; those long sleeps and wonderful figs.

—Patrick, Saint Mary Church, MN

Midday Prayer

I pray that those lost may find their way with the
light of God.

—Sarah, Holy Redeemer High School, PA

Evening Prayer

Dear Lord, please allow the pressures of my
teenage years to be eased by your Holy Spirit.

—Maria, Cardinal Spellman High School, MA

Morning Prayer

Lord, please help me to enhance and fulfill the gifts you have given me today.

—Nick, John Carroll High School, FL

Midday Prayer

Grant strength to those who are suffering in the world.

—Dominique, Saint Mary Church, MO

Evening Prayer

Thank you, God, for everything you do for me. I especially thank you for my family, because they love me very much.

—Briana, Cotter High School, MN

Morning Prayer

I want to be thankful. I pray to be thankful.

—Maria, Nerinx Hall High School, MO

Midday Prayer

Lord, be a shield for our troops in service.

—Dylan, Saints Peter and Paul High School, KS

Evening Prayer

God, help everyone to be strong and to stand up for what they believe in.

—Erin, Providence High School, IN

Morning Prayer

Lord, let me remember that it is okay to say no. Jesus said no.

—Sean, Our Mother of Mercy Church, TX

Midday Prayer

For those who find it hard to know their worth and purpose in the world, I pray to you, God.

—Elizabeth, Saint Francis Borgia Regional High School, MO

Evening Prayer

Dear Jesus, please show me what I look like in your loving eyes.

—Mary, Saint John High School, KS

Morning Prayer

Dear Lord, help me to carry out your will today.

—Matthew, Owensboro Catholic
High School, KY

Midday Prayer

I pray for those who are suffering mentally, physically, and spiritually, that they can overcome the obstacles that life has thrown at them.

—Hayley, DeLaSalle High School, MN

Evening Prayer

Bless all young people struggling with peer pressure.

—Tyler, Providence High School, IN

Morning Prayer

Lord, may I have the courage to stand up for you.

—John, Immaculate Conception Church, IA

Midday Prayer

I offer my prayer for people who haven't yet opened their hearts fully to God.

—Rebecca, Saint Peter Church, MO

Evening Prayer

Lord, when I am in doubt, help me to pray it out.

—Catherine, Saint Catherine Church, MA

Morning Prayer

Lord, help me to gather the courage to choose
your will and to inspire others to do the same.

—Ross, Saint Thomas More Church, KY

Midday Prayer

O God, I offer this prayer for all those who are
stressed with schoolwork.

—Jake, Saint Paul Church, NJ

Evening Prayer

God, give me the strength to live in this life, not
just exist.

—Jacob, Saint Francis Borgia Regional
High School, MO

Morning Prayer

God, thank you for always putting me first, even when I don't put you first.

—Mary, Cotter High School, MN

Midday Prayer

Blessed are all those who are bullied every day and are fighting to stay strong.

—Sam, Providence High School, IN

Evening Prayer

Lord, may everyone receive the love they deserve, I pray.

—Karly, Providence High School, IN

Morning Prayer

Good morning, God. Help me today to see how much you have given me.

—Josephine, Notre Dame-Cathedral Latin
High School, OH

Midday Prayer

For all aborted babies, I pray to you, Lord.

—Miranda, Saint Mary Church, MO

Evening Prayer

Help me to do what is right and help me to have the courage to stand up for what is right.

—Tyler, Saint Francis Borgia Regional
High School, MO

Morning Prayer

God, I pray that we can all learn how to do our best.

—Anton, DeLaSalle High School, MN

Midday Prayer

Bless, O Lord, all victims of cancer and those who are fighting to overcome this horrible disease.

—Kyle, Saint Francis Church, NE

Evening Prayer

Help me, Lord, to take in the information I've learned today and to use it to become a better person.

—John, Saint Apollinaris Church, CA

Morning Prayer

God, as I apply to college, help me to trust in your eternal love and to be open to your plan for me.

—Abby, Saint Rita Church, NY

Midday Prayer

Please bring Christian principles to all political leaders worldwide.

—Jack, Sacred Heart Church, IA

Evening Prayer

Dear Lord, help me to overcome the many harmful obstacles in our society today and to live out your will.

—Aubrey, Cotter High School, MN

Morning Prayer

Lord, help me to appreciate the wonder of your beautiful creation.

—Libby, Nerinx Hall High School, MO

Midday Prayer

For those who are affected by others' harmful words or actions, I pray to you, Lord.

—Nick, Saint Gabriel Church, IN

Evening Prayer

God, help me to realize that confusion is growth.

—Ashton, Saint Francis Borgia Regional High School, MO

Morning Prayer

God, help me to know that I'm always treasured
by you, even when I do not treasure myself.

—Grace, Good Shepherd Church, VA

Midday Prayer

Dear Lord, I pray for all the individuals who are
struggling with internal issues.

—Erica, Saint Mary Magdalen of
Pazzi Church, KY

Evening Prayer

Keep me safe from temptation. May your light
shine upon me and my peers.

—Jacob, John Carroll High School, FL

Morning Prayer

God, please give me the strength and courage to get through this day.

—Jenna, Holy Family Church, IN

Midday Prayer

I offer my prayer for tornado and tsunami victims.

—Maggie, Trinity Church, IA

Evening Prayer

God, please help me to love myself as much as I know you love me.

—Marissa, Saint Francis Borgia Regional High School, MO

Morning Prayer

Through all hard times, I know you keep me
protected and happy. Thank you, Lord.

—Ashley, Saint Mary Church, MI

Midday Prayer

I pray for everyone who is unsure of their faith.

—Briana, Saint Mary Church, KY

Evening Prayer

God, teach us to turn from violence and to turn
toward love.

—Jacob, Saint Mark Church, MI

Morning Prayer

Holy Father, keep my family safe in your loving arms.

—Michael, Saint Mary Church, MI

Midday Prayer

I offer this prayer, for the lives lost during international conflict.

—Emma, Saint Francis Xavier Church, GA

Evening Prayer

Lord, grant comfort to all those suffering from incurable diseases.

—Sarah, Saint Joseph Church, MI

Morning Prayer

Please help me to be the best friend I can be to everyone I meet.

—Maryann, Holy Family Church, IN

Midday Prayer

Thank you, Lord, for all volunteers.

—Javier, Christ the Good Shepherd Church, OH

Evening Prayer

God, protect me from my sins, and lead me to your path again.

—Barrett, Our Lady of Perpetual Help Church, IN

Morning Prayer

Lord, help me and all young people to spread your good and holy Word.

—Molly, Saint Pius X Church, IN

Midday Prayer

I pray for all those who have suffered loss, that they find hope in God.

—Sarah, IN

Evening Prayer

God, may I forgive those who have hurt me and those I care about.

—Katie, Saint Francis Borgia Regional
High School, MO

Morning Prayer

Lord, please give me the strength to live each day
to the fullest.

—Christina, Saint Elizabeth Church, TX

Midday Prayer

I pray for teenagers who are unsure what they
want to do after high school.

—Mary Anne, Washington Catholic
High School, IN

Evening Prayer

My prayer is for those who do not have God in
their lives, that they find you, Lord.

—Kat, Newman Catholic High School, WI

Morning Prayer

Lord, give me strength to let you take control so that I may follow your will today.

—Hannah, Cotter High School, MN

Midday Prayer

For vocations and everyone who is discerning God's plan for them, I pray.

—Laura, Mater Dei High School, IN

Evening Prayer

May those who often doubt themselves, Jesus, and others keep faithful and persevere through the challenges of life.

—Nathaniel, Saint Francis Borgia Regional High School, MO

Morning Prayer

Remind us, Lord, that you are everywhere we look,
even if we don't see you.

—Anonymous, Saint Catherine of
Alexandria, MA

Midday Prayer

For everyone in the world who has less than
others, I pray.

—Haley, Sacred Heart Church, IA

Evening Prayer

I offer my prayer for those who feel they have
sinned beyond forgiveness of God.

—Maegan, Sacred Heart Church, VA

Morning Prayer

Thank you, God, for this day on earth. May the world be filled with joy.

—Aidan, Cotter High School, MN

Midday Prayer

I offer this prayer for all who are facing surgery.

—Evan, Our Lady Queen of Peace Church, OH

Evening Prayer

Lord, protect my family till the end of our days, even when I cannot. Thank you, Father.

—Francisco, DeLaSalle High School, MN

Morning Prayer

Lord, help us to remember to not be afraid, for you are always with us.

—Emily, Saint John Vianney Church, MI

Midday Prayer

Dear God, please take care of the the ones who look down on themselves, and remind them that they are your children and therefore special.

—David, Saint Francis Borgia Regional High School, MO

Evening Prayer

My prayer is for those who cannot say what they want to say, those who cannot speak up and be heard.

—Lyliana, Saint Mary of Vernon Church, IL

Morning Prayer

God, please help me to see the world more clearly. Help me to see you clearly too.

—Isaiah, Cotter High School, MN

Midday Prayer

Dear Father, comfort families with those in the armed forces.

—Emily, Our Lady of Fátima Church, AR

Evening Prayer

I pray that all teens realize who they truly are and that they don't need fear in their lives.

—Brianna, Lourdes Church, IA

Morning Prayer

Lord, I pray for everyone who may be having a hard time, that they keep their heads held high.

—Samantha, Saint Francis Borgia Regional High School, MO

Midday Prayer

O God, please be with those who are suffering from mental illness.

—Maddie, Saint Margaret Mary Church, IL

Evening Prayer

I pray for any child who is sad.

—Tristan, Cotter High School, MN

Morning Prayer

Dear God, remind us that we should not be afraid to do the right thing, even when it's difficult.

—Nolan, La Salle High School, OH

Midday Prayer

Lord, help all young people who struggle in their relationship with their parents.

—Radey, Saint Benedict Church, OK

Evening Prayer

Thank you, Lord, for watching over my family, my friends, and me on a daily basis.

—Kara, Saint Francis Borgia Regional
High School, MO

Morning Prayer

God, please help us push through our fears and insecurities.

—Anonymous

Midday Prayer

Dear Father, bless those who are lost in this world.

—Patrycia, Saint Blasé Church, IL

Evening Prayer

I pray for those who have been hurt by others and themselves.

—Spencer, DeLaSalle High School, MN

Morning Prayer

May friends be there for us in hard times.

—Anonymous, Saint Francis Borgia Regional
High School, MO

Midday Prayer

Lord, I pray for all teens who are struggling with addiction.

—Toni, Saint Peter Church, MO

Evening Prayer

Dear God, thank you for the saints, popes, and patriarchs, for without them our religion would not be the same.

—Anonymous

Morning Prayer

Lord, allow each day I have to be filled with friends, and help me to keep those friends.

—Mollie, Saint Joseph Church, KY

Midday Prayer

I offer my prayer for all families and communities who are affected by fires.

—Tara, Our Lady of the Pines Church, CO

Evening Prayer

Dear God, when it is quiet and I am feeling sad, please send me someone to make me laugh.

—Imogen, Lourdes Hill College, Australia

Morning Prayer

Dear God, you are great.

—Anonymous

Midday Prayer

I pray for all families who must leave their homes and neighborhoods due to family issues.

—Katie, Saint Michael Church, MI

Evening Prayer

Lord, may everyone know that they are always loved by you and that you will forever be ready to comfort, support, guide, and teach us on our journey to Heaven.

—Stephanie, Notre Dame-Cathedral Latin High School, OH

Morning Prayer

Thank you, God, for everything you give to us.
Your love inspires us to give praise.

—Henry, Saint Mary Church, MN

Midday Prayer

For all of the seniors in high school who are
applying for college, I pray.

—Antonio, Saint Francis Cathedral, NJ

Evening Prayer

O God, let all those who seek, but find it hard to
discover, come to you and be filled with the Word
of your Son, through you.

—Alec, Notre Dame-Cathedral Latin
High School, OH

Morning Prayer

Help me to remember to pray for someone today.

—Emma, Good Shepherd Church, PA

Midday Prayer

I pray for farmers around the country and world.

—Mikayla, Immaculate Conception
Church, MO

Evening Prayer

I thought it was only the wind, but it was you.
Thank you, Lord.

—Zachary, Chaminade Julienne
High School, OH

Morning Prayer

May I remember today that everything is possible through Jesus Christ.

—Nancy, Saint James Church, IA

Midday Prayer

For those who don't think they are good enough, I offer this prayer.

—Emily, Saint Margaret Mary Church, IL

Evening Prayer

Lord, I pray that everyone in the world can find you.

—Hunter, Nativity of Our Lord Church, WI

Morning Prayer

Help us to make time for Jesus, put away
distractions to pray, and open up to you, Lord.

—Tony, Saint Therese Church, MI

Midday Prayer

Lord, I pray for students, that they use their best
abilities during midterms.

—Andrew, Saint Francis Borgia Regional
High School, MO

Evening Prayer

May all people around the world realize, God,
that you are always here.

—Mary, Saint Mary Church, MN

Morning Prayer

May we never stop dreaming. May we know that help is always around the corner and that you, God, are never far away.

—Lachlan, Marist College Canberra, Australia

Midday Prayer

Lord, please provide strength and perseverance to kids who get bullied.

—Kyle, Providence High School, IN

Evening Prayer

For the spirit of the young and old, I pray.

—Matt, Saint Patrick Church, IA

Morning Prayer

This day may I give my best for your greater glory, O God.

—Isaiah, Xavier High School, NY

Midday Prayer

God, may you bless those who are discerning their vocation. Lord, please help them to follow your path for them.

—Tommy, Saint Paul the Apostle Church, IL

Evening Prayer

Help me to stay close to you, God, at all times. May you give me wisdom to do what is right and just.

—Sarah, Good Shepherd Church, VA

Morning Prayer

Today help me, Lord, to take the time to
appreciate the beauty of the world around us.

—Christian, Saint Thérèse of Lisieux Church, MI

Midday Prayer

For all those fighting for our country, God, thank
you for their bravery. Please keep them safe.

—Becca, Immaculate Heart of Mary Church, IN

Evening Prayer

Lord, I pray for our sufferings, for only you can
help us persevere through them.

—Clara, Saint Ludmila Church, IA

Morning Prayer

Lord, follow and guide me through tough times,
and share with me the happiness of knowing you.

—Jarrod, Marist College Canberra, Australia

Midday Prayer

For all women and children who are being
abused, I pray to you, Lord.

—Luke, Guardian Angels Central
High School, NE

Evening Prayer

Thank you, God, for my friends, my family, and
my health. I ask you to help me stay strong in my
darkest times.

—Frannie, Cotter High School, MN

Morning Prayer

Lord, fill us with joy from the little things in our lives, that each moment can be an instance of happiness.

—Cameron, DeLaSalle High School, MN

Midday Prayer

Lord, I pray for society's safety.

—Shay, Saint Elizabeth of Hungary
High School, TX

Evening Prayer

God, let me find the up side, even when things are looking down.

—Carrie, Saint Francis Borgia Regional
High School, MO

Morning Prayer

May I lead others to invite Jesus into their hearts.

—Alison, Nativity of Our Lord Church, WI

Midday Prayer

Lord, help all the innocent people who have to suffer because of terrorism.

—Fred, Sacred Heart of Jesus Church, OH

Evening Prayer

I pray for those without hope for the future. Help them, God, to have a dream.

—Kathleen, Sacred Heart Church, VA

Morning Prayer

Lord, may I and all those I love find joy in everyday life.

—Benjamin, Saint Elizabeth of Hungary
High School, TX

Midday Prayer

I pray, Lord, that you watch over the many needy people in the world and be their everlasting Savior.

—Emma, Saint Mary Church, IA

Evening Prayer

Dear Lord, thank you for everything you have done for your children.

—Erin, Providence High School, IN

Morning Prayer

Thank you for the gift of your Son, Jesus Christ.

—Laura, Saint Anthony Church, TX

Midday Prayer

Today I pray for those who are hungry and suffering in their times of need.

—Cailey, Saint John Neumann Church, MD

Evening Prayer

Help me to seek you, Lord, the way the wise ones sought the infant Jesus in the manger.

—Kylie, Saint James Church, NY

Morning Prayer

Dear God, thank you for my life. I will try to live up to your words.

—Emily, Cotter High School, MN

Midday Prayer

God of compassion, I pray for those who have no one to pray for them.

—Rachel, Saint Brigid Church, MI

Evening Prayer

I pray for the happiness of my parents and all parents.

—Isa, Saint Elizabeth of Hungary
High School, TX

Morning Prayer

God, let me remember that you nourish me and all
of life.

—Grey, Notre Dame-Cathedral Latin
High School, OH

Midday Prayer

Lord, heal all those who are sick or in pain.

—Alyssa, Providence High School, IN

Evening Prayer

I pray that the sun may shine on the darkest souls.

—Brianna, Saint Francis Borgia Regional
High School, MO

Morning Prayer

God, please help me to keep hope despite all the chaos in our world.

—Annie, Saint Andrew Church, OH

Midday Prayer

Lord, please be with everyone who is struggling with their own self confidence.

—Janie, Saint Francis Borgia Regional High School, MO

Evening Prayer

May all of our brothers and sisters, in every part of the world, grow up and achieve thier goals.

—Brendan, Marist College Canberra, Australia

Morning Prayer

Thank you, Lord, for this day and the people in it. I would like to pray for those who need help and those who are very sick.

—Tyler, Cotter High School, MN

Midday Prayer

Help us to reach out to the poor and the homeless in the world.

—Ben, Immaculate Conception Church, IA

Evening Prayer

Dear Lord, love is not tangible, though it is just simply perfection. Amen.

—Luke, Marist College Canberra, Australia

Morning Prayer

May we not just forgive and forget; help us to forgive and be transformed.

—Lauren, Saints Simon and Jude Church, TX

Midday Prayer

I offer this prayer for those who are struggling in the world and have no one to turn to.

—Carmelito, Holy Family Church, CO

Evening Prayer

Dear Lord, thank you for everything. I am so grateful for my family, friends, and everybody around me that has affected my life.

—Gabby, Cotter High School, MN

Morning Prayer

Let us pray for love to spread across the world.

—Matthew, DeLaSalle High School, MN

Midday Prayer

God, please help to bring comfort to all the people in need of your saving.

—Kenzie, Sacred Heart of Jesus Church, OH

Evening Prayer

Mother Mary, help us to grow closer to Jesus, your Son, who so loved us to give his life for us.

—Libby, Good Shepherd Church, KS

Index of Themes

Reflections are provided for each of the following themes, which can be located by turning to the corresponding calendar dates.

Abortion: Jan 7, Feb 3, Feb 27, Jul 15, Aug 2, Aug 21, Nov 22

Abuse: Mar 1, Jun 27, Sep 7, Sep 26, Oct 11, Dec 10, Dec 21

Acceptance: Jan 7, Jan 12, Feb 1, Feb 13, Feb 22, Feb 28, Mar 6, Apr 2, Apr 24, May 3, Jun 14, Jun 29, Aug 5, Sep 13, Sep 21

Addictions: Jan 4, May 25, Jun 16, Sep 14, Nov 8, Dec 11

Anger: Feb 9, Sep 7, Nov 10

Animals: Feb 8, Jun 1, Jun 9, Jul 16

Anxiety: Feb 24, Mar 23, Jul 10

Appearance: Jan 29, Aug 18

Appreciation: Jan 24, Jan 26, Feb 12, Mar 19, May 4, Aug 22, Sep 18, Nov 22, Nov 25, Dec 20

Attitude: Mar 15, Apr 3, Dec 22

Authenticity: Jan 13, Jan 21, Feb 13, Feb 25, Mar 9, Mar 23, Mar 31, Apr 6, Apr 10, Apr 30, Jun 12, Jul 18, Jul 20, Jul 25, Jul 26, Aug 9, Sep 13, Oct 17, Oct 27, Nov 4, Dec 7

Autism: Feb 11

Bullying: Jan 26, Feb 22, Mar 4, Apr 10, Apr 13, Apr 16, Apr 18, Jun 13, Jul 30, Sep 9, Oct 9, Oct 20, Nov 21, Nov 25, Dec 18

Cancer: Feb 6, Feb 21, Mar 24, May 1, May 11, Jul 4, Aug 14, Oct 3, Nov 23

Change: Jun 11, Sep 9

Children: Mar 26, Apr 23, Apr 29, May 28, Jul 6, Jul 13, Aug 24, Aug 30, Sep 16, Sep 22, Sep 27, Oct 3, Oct 11, Oct 14, Oct 21

Christian Living: Jan 28, Feb 4, Feb 11, Feb 14, Feb 16, Mar 2, Apr 9, Aug 29, Oct 21

Church Community: Jun 3, Aug 13, Sep 21, Oct 24

College: Jul 17, Aug 25, Nov 24, Dec 14

Commitment: Jan 16, Feb 14, Sep 4

Communication: Jan 20, Feb 6, Mar 17, Dec 6

Compassion: May 25, Aug 5, Sep 2, Dec 26

Confidence: Jan 18, Feb 9, Feb 18, Aug 11, Oct 30, Dec 28

Confirmation: Jun 2

Confusion: Jul 19, Aug 7, Nov 13, Nov 25

Courage: Jan 5, Jan 9, Jan 11, Jan 14, Jan 21, Feb 15, Feb 17, Mar 4, Mar 27, Apr 10, May 11, Jul 28, Sep 18, Oct 19, Nov 19, Nov 20, Nov 22, Nov 27

Creation: Mar 13, Mar 30, Jul 26, Aug 22, Sep 29, Nov 25

Death: Jan 16, Feb 10, Jun 21, Aug 30, Sep 12, Oct 29. *See also* **Grief**

Decision Making: Jan 8, Jan 20, Feb 4, Feb 5, Feb 13, Mar 15, Apr 6, Apr 8, May 30, May 31, June 18, Jul 22, Jul 26, Sep 16, Nov 13, Nov 17, Nov 22, Dec 19

Depression: Jan 18, Feb 2, Mar 8, Apr 22, May 2, Jul 10, Jul 30, Aug 11

Disabilities: Apr 24, Aug 14, Aug 24

Diversity: Feb 28, Mar 26, Apr 24, May 3, Aug 5, Aug 8, Aug 13, Sep 2

Divorce: Mar 25, Oct 19

Doubt: Feb 5, May 4, May 22, Jun 16, Jul 20, Oct 14, Nov 19, Nov 28, Dec 3

Drought: Aug 6

Eating Disorders: Sep 4

Education. *See* **School**

Enemies: Jan 28, Feb 21, Aug 4, Oct 20, Nov 3

Failure: Aug 14, Sep 9, Sep 12, Sep 21

Faith: Jan 2, Jan 5, Jan 6, Jan 14, Jan 17, Jan 18, Feb 2, Feb 10, Feb 15, Feb 19, Mar 4, Mar 7, Mar 11, Mar 19, Apr 15, Apr 17, Apr 18, Apr 25, Apr 27, May 10, May 31, Jun 6, Jun 7, Jun 20, Jun 21, Jun 23, Jul 18, Jul 31, Aug 29, Oct 3, Oct 17, Nov 28

Faithfulness: Mar 3, Apr 26, Aug 2, Sep 15, Sep 24, Oct 30, Dec 3

Faithless: Jan 28, Feb 4, Feb 16, Feb 19, Jun 3, Jun 7, Jul 28, Aug 1, Aug 6, Aug 9, Sep 30, Oct 5, Oct 7, Oct 16, Nov 19, Dec 2, Dec 16

Faith Sharing: Jan 9, Jan 12, Feb 17, Feb 21, Mar 2, Mar 27, Apr 10, Apr 23, May 30, Jun 20, Jun 25, Sep 13, Oct 15, Dec 1, Dec 23

Family: Jan 2, Feb 8, Feb 9, Feb 14, Feb 20, Mar 13, Mar 16, Mar 17, Mar 18, Mar 19, Mar 28, Apr 19, May 23, Jun 8, Jun 10, Jun 16, Jun 20, Jul 6, Jul 7, Jul 8, Jul 10, Jul 12, Jul 13, Aug 2, Aug 3, Aug 10, Aug 18, Aug 29, Sep 17, Sep 19, Oct 2, Oct 4, Oct 21, Nov 15, Nov 29, Dec 5, Dec 9, Dec 13

Farmers: Dec 15

Fear: Jan 8, Jan 21, Feb 24, Feb 25, Mar 10, Mar 16, Mar 17, Mar 18, Mar 20, Mar 21, Mar 22, Mar 23, Apr 7, Apr 15, Apr 22, Apr 25, Apr 28, Apr 29, May 1, Jun 4, Jun 6, Jul 12, Sep 12, Sep 28, Oct 22,

Oct 26, Dec 6, Dec 7, Dec 9, Dec 10

Fires: Dec 12

Focus: Jan 4, Jan 20, Apr 26, Jun 5, Jul 4, Oct 10

Forgiveness: Feb 11, Apr 9, Apr 26, May 20, May 29, Jun 14, Jul 8, Aug 31, Sep 3, Oct 31, Dec 1, Dec 4, Dec 30

Foster Children: Apr 29

Friendship: Jan 11, Feb 4, Feb 12, Feb 14, Feb 15, Feb 22, Mar 13, Mar 25, Mar 27, Mar 28, Mar 29, Apr 4, Apr 14, May 5, May 8, May 9, May 12, May 23, Jun 7, Jun 20, Jul 1, Jul 12, Jul 25, Aug 1, Aug 25, Sep 18, Oct 4, Oct 25, Nov 30, Dec 9, Dec 11, Dec 12

Frustration: Nov 13

Future: Jan 19, Jan 20, Jan 21, Jan 22, Mar 24, Apr 6, Jun 5, Jul 5, Jul 14, Jul 19, Jul 22, Aug 7, Dec 2, Dec 23

God: Feb 10, Feb 18, Mar 3, Mar 19, Apr 12, May 6, May 7, May 12, May 22, Aug 1, Aug 30, Sep 3, Oct 18, Nov 1, Dec 13, Dec 17

God's Image: Jan 6, Jan 13, May 30, Jul 24

God's Love: Jan 1, Jan 3, Jan 29, Apr 28, May 6, May 8, May 17, May 22, May 24, May 25, Jun 14, Aug 19, Aug 20, Sep 13, Sep 26, Oct 1, Oct 14, Oct 25, Nov 1, Nov 3, Dec 13, Dec 14

God's Plan/Will: Jan 11, Jan 23, Feb 1, Feb 15, Mar 7, Mar 10, Mar 28, Apr 2, Apr 18, Jun 22, Jun 25, Jul 2, Jul 3, Aug 15, Sep 4, Sep 5, Sep 22, Sep 28, Sep 30, Oct 5, Oct 10, Oct 26, Oct 29, Nov 11, Nov 18, Nov 20, Nov 24, Dec 3, Dec 19

God's Presence: Jan 9, Jan 11, Jan 15, Jan 19, Jan 24, Jan 29, Feb 2, Feb 28, Mar 8, Mar 15, Mar 22,

Apr 19, Apr 30, May 6, May 7, Jun 2, Jun 10, Jun 11, Jun 13, Jun 14, Jun 22, Jun 23, Jul 19, Sep 27, Oct 5, Oct 12, Oct 17, Oct 19, Nov 2, Dec 4, Dec 6, Dec 17, Dec 18

Grandparents: Feb 7, Mar 24, May 8, Jul 6, Aug 11

Grief: Mar 14, May 5, Jun 26, Jul 5, Aug 30, Sep 16, Sep 26, Oct 15, Oct 24

Guidance: Jan 27, Feb 3, Feb 29, Mar 2, Mar 11, Mar 16, Mar 21, Mar 29, Apr 11, May 16, May 17, Jun 21, Jun 27, Jul 5, Jul 23, Jul 26, Aug 5, Aug 19, Sep 10, Sep 20, Sep 30, Oct 3, Oct 8, Nov 4, Dec 21

Happiness: Jan 18, Jan 25, Feb 24, Mar 8, Mar 31, Apr 1, Apr 13, Apr 20, May 7, May 25, Jun 1, Jun 3, Jun 5, Jul 4, Jul 5, Jul 11, Jul 12, Aug 12, Aug 21, Aug 22, Sep 17, Oct 12, Oct 13, Oct 28, Nov 11, Nov 28, Dec 5, Dec 22,

Dec 24, Dec 26

Hardships: Jan 3, Jan 13, Jan 17, Feb 4, Feb 8, Feb 23, Mar 1, Mar 7, Mar 13, Mar 19, Apr 1, Apr 2, Apr 13, Apr 15, Apr 17, Apr 20, Apr 30, May 13, May 14, May 15, May 21, May 28, Jun 2, Jul 14, Jul 22, Jul 27, Jul 30, Aug 4, Aug 18, Aug 19, Sep 2, Sep 4, Sep 17, Sep 19, Sep 20, Sep 21, Oct 11, Oct 12, Oct 23, Oct 29, Nov 12, Nov 18, Nov 28, Dec 8, Dec 11

Health Care Workers: Apr 21, Oct 27

Heaven: Jan 31, Mar 12, May 12, Dec 13

Homelessness: Jan 31, Feb 5, Feb 16, Feb 24, Jun 29, Aug 10, Aug 15, Aug 19, Sep 2, Sep 25, Oct 1, Oct 22, Oct 31, Nov 11, Dec 29

Honesty: Aug 26

Hope: Jan 14, Jan 17, Jan 30, Mar 29, Mar 30,

Apr 11, May 9, May 13, May 15, May 29, Jun 13, Jul 4, Jul 17, Aug 4, Aug 10, Sep 28, Dec 1, Dec 23, Dec 28

Humility: Jul 28, Aug 21, Sep 16

Hunger: Feb 5, Feb 23, Feb 24, Jun 9, Nov 13, Dec 25

Illness. *See* **Sickness**

Inclusion: Feb 13, Apr 24, Jun 14

Individuality: May 2

Jesus: Jul 10, Jul 11, Oct 4, Oct 25, Oct 31, Dec 16, Dec 25, Dec 31

Joy. *See* **Happiness**

Judgment: Nov 8

Justice: Feb 29, May 18, Aug 5, Sep 8, Sep 11, Nov 22

Kindness: Jan 10, Apr 4, Jul 2, Oct 6

Leadership: Jan 30, Mar 20, Jun 18, Sep 3, Nov 24, Dec 11

Loneliness: Jan 24, May 17, Jul 2, Jul 20, Aug 18, Aug 22, Sep 21, Oct 24

Lost: Jan 5, Jan 27, Feb 19, May 17, May 18, May 29, Jun 7, Jun 30, Aug 5, Aug 9, Aug 20, Aug 27, Oct 14, Nov 14, Dec 10

Love: Jan 10, Jan 22, Jan 23, Jan 25, Feb 24, Feb 26, Mar 6, Mar 9, Mar 24, Apr 2, Apr 3, Apr 7, Apr 14, Apr 19, Apr 21, Apr 23, May 1, May 5, May 9, May 19, May 21, May 22, May 24, May 27, May 28, Jun 8, Jun 11, Jul 2, Jul 16, Aug 2, Aug 12, Aug 31, Sep 16, Sep 21, Oct 3, Oct 6, Oct 11, Oct 20, Nov 5, Nov 21, Nov 27, Nov 28, Dec 29, Dec 31. *See also* **God's Love**

Marriage: Jan 22, Mar 9, Apr 25, Jun 17, Jul 1, Aug 11, Sep 16, Oct 10

Mental Illness: Apr 22, Jul 23, Oct 1, Oct 30, Nov 7, Nov 26, Dec 8

Military Personnel: Jan 19, Jan 27, Apr 19, May 17, Jun 15, Jun 23, Jul 11, Jul 27, Aug 21, Aug 26, Aug 31, Sep 29, Oct 7, Nov 16, Dec 7, Dec 20

Money: Jun 24, Aug 17

Musicians: Jul 31

Natural Disasters: Feb 17, May 16, Jun 11, Jul 7, Aug 3, Sep 15, Oct 4, Oct 18, Nov 13, Nov 27

Needy people: Mar 31, Apr 7, May 21, Jul 17, Jul 31, Aug 23, Aug 26, Sep 14, Oct 16, Oct 28, Nov 2, Nov 6, Nov 11, Dec 4, Dec 24, Dec 29

New Experiences: Feb 19, Jun 4

Oppression: Jun 28

Organization: Aug 1

Pain: Jan 15, Mar 16, May 9, Jul 3, Aug 29, Sep 10, Sep 18, Nov 9, Dec 27

Parents: Feb 6, Feb 10, Apr 3, May 3, May 20, Aug 12, Aug 28, Aug 29, Sep 8, Oct 21, Dec 9, Dec 26

Patience: Feb 11, Mar 26, Aug 4, Sep 16

Peace: Jan 18, Feb 27, Apr 2, Apr 19, Apr 30, Jul 13, Jul 14, Jul 30, Aug 7, Aug 12, Aug 20, Aug 28, Sep 11, Oct 13, Oct 19, Oct 28, Nov 12

Peer Pressure: Jan 6, Mar 23, Jun 9, Jul 3, Aug 9, Nov 4, Nov 18

Perfection: Mar 6, Jul 19

Perseverance: May 15, Jun 4, Oct 23, Dec 3, Dec 20

Poor: Jan 1, May 18, Jul 28, Sep 25, Dec 29

Priesthood: Jul 29, Sep 24

Procrastination: Apr 20

Protection: Jan 5, Feb 18, Mar 12, May 4, Jun 1, Jun 12, Jun 17, Jun 19, Sep 1, Nov 28, Dec 5

Purgatory: Sep 22

Relationships: Jan 20, Jan 23, Mar 1, Mar 6, May 19, Jul 9

Religious Persecution: Sep 23

Respectfulness: Jan 10, Jan 14, Jan 16, Mar 26, May 12, Aug 27, Oct 26

Sadness: Jan 25, Mar 14, Jul 12, Jul 30, Sep 6, Sep 9, Sep 11, Oct 12, Dec 8, Dec 12. *See also* **Grief**

Safety: Jan 8, Mar 27, Apr 29, May 13, May 23, May 26, Jun 9, Jun 10, Jun 11, Jun 16, Jun 19, Aug 20, Aug 29, Aug 31, Sep 10, Sep 17, Sep 23, Nov 29, Dec 20, Dec 22

Saints: Sep 1, Dec 11

School: Jan 3, Jan 7, Jan 22, Feb 1, Feb 20, Mar 2, Apr 4, Apr 8, Apr 19, Apr 27, May 14, May 20, May 23, May 26, Jun 9, Jun 30, Jul 21, Aug 24, Sep 5, Sep 6, Sep 10, Sep 25, Oct 8,

Oct 23, Nov 6, Nov 20, Dec 17

Self-Esteem: Feb 18, Apr 23, Apr 28, Jul 2, Jul 15, Jul 21, Jul 23, Jul 24, Jul 25, Jul 27, Aug 1, Aug 11, Aug 15, Oct 22, Nov 9, Nov 17, Dec 6, Dec 16

Self-Improvement: Mar 26

Selflessness: Feb 27, Jul 16

Self-Respect: Apr 2, Oct 17

Service: Jan 1, Jan 7, Apr 7, Jun 6, Jun 14, Jul 29, Aug 7, Aug 17, Aug 20, Aug 21, Sep 19, Oct 6, Nov 10, Nov 30

Sexuality: Jan 22, Jan 28, Apr 15, Jun 19

Sickness: Feb 7, Mar 11, Mar 14, Apr 17, Apr 29, May 1, Jun 17, Jul 2, Jul 8, Jul 24, Aug 3, Aug 8, Aug 13, Aug 24, Sep 1, Sep 5, Sep 6, Oct 1, Oct 7, Oct 16, Oct 21, Oct 31,

Nov 3, Nov 13, Nov 29, Dec 27, Dec 29. *See also specific types of illnesses*

Sin: Jul 28, Aug 6, Sep 5, Nov 30, Dec 4

Sleep: Mar 22, Aug 16

Solidarity: Mar 5, Jun 14, Jun 15, Aug 8, Aug 22

Sports: Mar 20, Nov 5

Strength: Jan 11, Jan 13, Jan 23, Jan 25, Jan 31, Feb 8, Feb 16, Feb 28, Feb 29, Mar 7, Mar 10, Apr 14, May 11, May 14, May 30, Jun 8, Jun 24, Jun 26, Jul 24, Sep 20, Oct 2, Oct 13, Nov 9, Nov 10, Nov 15, Nov 16, Nov 20, Nov 27, Dec 2

Stress: Jul 20, Nov 14

Success: Feb 7, Feb 23, Mar 5, Mar 15, Apr 11, Apr 26, May 14, Jun 3, Oct 6, Dec 28

Suffering: Jan 3, Jan 6, Jan 12, Jan 15, Feb 2, Feb 8, Mar 1, Mar 16, Apr 12, May 9, May 19, Jul 1,

Jul 3, Jul 17, Jul 28, Aug 16, Aug 19, Aug 23, Aug 24, Aug 29, Sep 1, Sep 18, Sep 19, Sep 20, Sep 23, Sep 24, Nov 9, Nov 15, Nov 18

Suicide: Apr 10, Apr 13, Apr 18, Apr 22, Jun 22

Support: Jan 30, May 26, May 28, Aug 2, Oct 25

Surgery: Aug 28, Dec 5

Talents: Jan 9, Jul 29, Oct 15

Teachers: Nov 6

Temptation: May 31, Jun 27, Nov 10, Nov 13, Nov 24, Nov 26, Nov 30

Thankfulness: Jan 1, Jan 2, Jan 4, Jan 10, Jan 17, Jan 24, Feb 17, Feb 26, Mar 14, Mar 25, Mar 30, Apr 4, Apr 8, Apr 26, Apr 28, May 3, May 10, May 11, May 18, May 19, May 23, May 28, Jun 8, Jul 5, Jul 9, Jul 11, Aug 16, Aug 17, Aug 23, Aug 28, Oct 9, Oct 18, Nov 2, Nov 4,

Nov 7, Nov 14, Nov 15, Nov 16, Dec 21, Dec 24, Dec 26, Dec 30

Travel: Jan 8, May 13

Trust in God: Jan 17, Jan 19, Jan 31, Feb 14, Apr 18, Apr 22, Apr 24, May 25, Aug 2, Oct 17, Oct 23, Nov 2

Unborn Children: Apr 23, Jul 6

Unity: Mar 12, Aug 8, Oct 3

Values and Virtues: Feb 9, Feb 14, Feb 23, Apr 6

Violence: Feb 26, Mar 23, Mar 26, Mar 28, May 4, Jul 13, Aug 25, Sep 7, Sep 10, Sep 20, Sep 27, Sep 28, Sep 29, Oct 2, Oct 28, Nov 13, Nov 28, Nov 29, Dec 23. *See also* **Abuse**

Vocations: Jun 5, Jul 17, Jul 22, Oct 2, Oct 5, Oct 27, Dec 3, Dec 19

Voiceless People: Jan 17, Jan 20, Feb 6, Mar 17, Apr 5, Jun 10, Jul 6, Jul 21, Sep 15, Sep 20, Dec 6

Wisdom: Sep 16, Dec 19

Work: Jan 23, Sep 8

Worry: Mar 20, Jun 5, Nov 7